D0469297

BOOKS BY GAY HENDRICKS

Learning to Love Yourself
Learning to Love Yourself Workbook
The Centering Book (with Russel Wills)

BOOKS BY GAY HENDRICKS
AND KATHLYN HENDRICKS

Centering & the Art of Intimacy
Conscious Loving

Centering and the Art of Intimacy Handbook

A New Psychology of Close Relationships

Gay Hendricks, Ph.D. and
Kathlyn Hendricks, Ph.D.

A Fireside Book
Published by Simon & Schuster
New York London Toronto Sydney Tokyo Singapore

FIRESIDE

Rockefeller Center
1230 Avenue of the Americas
New York, New York 10020

Designed by Richard Oriolo
Manufactured in the United States of America

10 9 8 7 6 5 4 3 2

Library of Congress Cataloging-in-Publication Data
Hendricks, Gay.
Centering and the art of intimacy handbook : a new psychology of close relationships / Gay Hendricks, Kathlyn Hendricks.
p. cm.
Companion vol. to: Centering and the art of intimacy.
Includes index.
1. Intimacy (Psychology) 2. Centering (Psychology) 3. Interpersonal relations.
I. Hendricks, Kathlyn. II. Title.
BF575.I5H462 1993
158′.2—dc20 92-35482
CIP

ISBN: 0-671-76719-4

Contents

Part One

A New Psychology of Close Relationships

Introduction: In the Laboratory of the Human Heart

....

This book has been written in a time of unprecedented opportunity for growth in relationships. Walls have crumbled all over the world, including in the realm of human interaction. If anything is clear in this changing world, it is that relationships are desperately in need of transformation. The game has changed; now a new set of rules must be created.

The transformation of relationships has consumed the interest of the authors for many years. Based on our two-and-a-half decades of experience in counseling couples and single people, we have developed a psychology of close relationships that moves people toward greater harmony and creativity. Our book *Centering & the Art of Intimacy* laid out the theory, and now we offer the workbook to help our readers put it into practice. We offer you the essence of what we have found works best in workbook format because we want to put these new techniques directly into your hands. The material is written so that the individual, as well as the group member or leader, can easily use the activities and ideas presented.

The old saying tells us that there is nothing new under the sun, but in light of the miracles we have seen couples accomplish in their relationships over the past two decades, the old saying might just be wrong. There has been so much learned in the psychology of relationships in the past several decades that we, the authors, are in awe of and made hopeful by the transformative possibilities now open to all of us.

AN ERA OF INTENSE CHANGE

Relationships have changed utterly and enormously in recent years—some would say for the worse, others for the better. From our perspective as relationship therapists, we say yes to both points of view. Those who are committed to changing their relationships are soaring to new highs, while those who resist changing are finding the ground buckling beneath them.

In technological societies, relationships seem to be the final frontier. We have gone to the moon, but have yet to map out the territory of the human heart. It is sobering to visit Tokyo and New York and see the clash between space-age technology and stone-age human communication. How could a species that can build a jet plane or a bullet train be so obtuse in their close relationships? How can a scientist who ponders the mysteries of cold fusion by day go home at night and be so inept at the warmer fusion of family life? Never before has there been such a gap, and never such a crying need to bridge it. Unless the gap between technology and communication in relationships is healed, the human experiment on this planet may be doomed.

A Window on Relationships

As therapists, we have a window on communication that is unique. We are present to the worst and best in human interaction, as well as everything in between. For example, we counseled a couple who had not exchanged a kind word, much less a tender caress, for several months. In an hour of intense, carefully guided communication, they said things to each other that have been hidden beneath the surface, unknown even to themselves. They were healed and left our office hand in hand. Another couple came to us in similar tight-lipped silence, but their efforts to communicate fell short. They left as much or more estranged as when they came in. Perhaps another day will herald a breakthrough for them, but until then they remain stuck. It is in this laboratory of the human heart that the ideas and activities in this workbook were conceived and tested. What is presented here for your use has passed the test of helping real people heal their very real relationship problems.

As practicing therapists, we are faced with the problem of relieving immediate pain. People come to us to feel better, to improve their lives and their relationships. People do not pay therapists to develop theories. However, as authors and contributors to the development of the profession, we have a strong interest in developing a useful and testable theory of relationship therapy. Our theory was developed from the inside out. By cataloging the various techniques that led couples to greater happiness and harmony, we gradually compiled a catalog of interventions that worked. As this catalog grew, a theory emerged. The interventions organized themselves into coherent categories, suggesting a powerful new theory that will keep researchers busy for a long time.

Our Own Relationship

Our relationship has been both proving ground and direct beneficiary of the concepts and processes described in this and our earlier book. We met and married at the beginning of the eighties. Now, well into the nineties and the second decade of our marriage, we are deeply grateful for the amount of love and creative energy that the ideas expressed here have given us. We live and breathe these concepts every day of our lives. We use them in our work and in our relations with family and friends. Used skillfully, they are the foundations of a very powerful approach to living. The fundamentals—awareness, honesty, commitment—can be applied anywhere in our lives. In normal human existence, these simple things are often more conspicuous by their absence than their presence. But when they are practiced and held high as the standard, they provide a beacon to guide us in our journey toward better relationships.

Our relationship has become a source of ongoing fun and spiritual growth, far beyond our initial hopes and dreams. As therapists, the ideas in the book have become the backbone of our entire approach to helping our clients. We appreciate your interest and commitment to relationship growth and invite you to participate wholeheartedly in this work with us.

CHAPTER ONE

The Essentials of Close Relationships

......

You can learn either by wisdom or experience. There is nothing wrong with learning through experience—in fact, there are plenty of things that can only be learned that way. Try learning to make love or hit a golf ball solely by thinking about it and reading the instruction manual! But there are lots of other things that can best be learned through wisdom and by taking a careful look at the rules and regulations before going into the field of play. Learning to cross the street is one area in which learning by wisdom and not solely by experience is preferable. Few of us would be here if our parents had said, "Just go out in the street and experiment. See if you can find something that works." Yet that is the way we frequently enter the realm of relationships.

Too many of us make the same mistakes over and over in

relationships. Some wise person once pointed out that life is not one thing after the other, it is often the same thing over and over again. Nowhere is this problem more acute than in relationships. Some of you may remember the popular TV movie of a few years back that starred Farrah Fawcett as a woman who poured gasoline over her abusive husband and torched him as he slept. It was based on a true story, and, predictably, much publicity ensued. In the movie the woman was depicted as a victim and a heroine who dared to strike back after years of beatings and abuse. However, practically no attention was paid to the real-life woman on whom the story was based. Not long after the movie appeared, she married another abusive man, who allegedly molested her daughter. As therapists, we see examples week in and week out of people who are unconsciously repeating the same patterns in one relationship after another.

We would like to illustrate this problem with an example from our own relationship. In the first year we were together we found ourselves recognizing patterns that we had seen in our past relationships. One of the most troublesome patterns was one that we have since seen many other couples repeat. We would get close to each other, then find some way to destroy the closeness. At the end of a busy week, with a long weekend of potential closeness ahead of us, we would get into some kind of wrangle on Friday night. Then Saturday and Sunday would be spent sorting it out. As we looked into the source of this problem, we both learned crucial things about ourselves. First we had to acknowledge that it was not anybody's fault. Although we were both firmly convinced that it was the other person's fault, we realized that we each had to take complete responsibility and not blame the other person. When we stopped focusing on blame we had more insight into which of our own dynamics were causing the problem. In Gay's case, he found that he had a lot of fear that would emerge when he got close. To avoid dealing with the fear, he would get angry. Kathlyn would assume that she had done something wrong to provoke Gay's anger. She would be scared of his anger and would try to be inconspicuous. Naturally, these patterns prevented any possibility for intimacy.

During our first year we made an agreement that has served us very well. We decided that we were going to tell the whole truth and nothing but the truth to each other. We were not going to edit or sort the truth, but instead go to great lengths to say anything we had going on in our minds or bodies. Some people might think this would be boring, but to us it was endlessly fascinating. As we became skilled at telling the truth we made remarkable discoveries about how much we had withheld the truth in past relationships. Gay discovered that he had been using anger to mask his fears for most of his life, while Kathlyn learned that she had been hiding from men's anger at least since she was four or five years old. By speaking the truth we were able to talk about these patterns until we understood them and ceased to repeat them with each other.

THE TWIN NEEDS FOR UNITY AND AUTONOMY

By exploring issues like this one we learned one of the great truths of relationships. People have deep needs for closeness and for separateness. We yearn for unity with another person, and we also yearn for complete individuation, the development of freedom, autonomy, and a personal connection with the world. Both of these needs are absolutely fundamental, but they are also fraught with difficulties. Most of us have had painful experiences with getting close and with getting separate. We have been wounded trying to achieve one or both states. At some time, possibly even in the first few minutes of life, something may have happened that established a flinch reaction to getting close. Later, during the development of our autonomy, we may have experienced events that kept us from its full expression.

Certainly traumas cause flinches, but they are not the only cause for our difficulties in close relationships. Slow learning, in the form of things we see going on around us over time, is just as likely to cause flinching. For example, Gay grew up in a family where there was little touching. He remembers being surprised to see his grandfather touch his grandmother's arm at the funeral of her brother and recalling that it was the first time he had ever seen them touch. Later this showed up in his relationships in several ways. Kathlyn grew up in a much more touch-oriented family. In early courtship, Kathlyn would take Gay's arm out in public, and he would notice a wave of discomfort.

The growth of a close relationship resembles the early stages of childhood development. The infant's task when it arrives here on earth is quite simple: Being. It must master the art of being close to another person and getting its needs met. If all is untroubled in the primary relationship (nearly always with the mother), the infant will learn that this is a place where it can get its needs met. Later in the first year of life, separation occurs as the infant learns its second major lesson: Doing. The infant, in its second six months of life, learns to explore and to act on the environment in a variety of ways.

The parallels found in later close relationships are very clear. During the initial stages of a close relationship, the emphasis is on Being. We are learning whether this is a person we can trust. Can we get our needs met here? Usually there is great emphasis on body contact and being together in essential ways: eating, sleeping, dancing, walking. Then a movement toward autonomy begins. We need to find out if this is a relationship in which we can experience both unity with another person and the development of ourselves as separate beings. Can we be close and be ourselves at the same time?

Into this key period rushes the power of our past conditioning. As therapists, we cannot count the times we have heard something like this: "For the first few months everything was great, then everything seemed to change overnight. Suddenly she/he seemed to change personalities." It is as if the closeness we achieve in the first stages of a relationship flashes a signal to some part of our minds that says, "Time to bring out the hidden aspects of you!" At this point the controlling side of ourselves, or the dependent, or the violent, emerges, and the power struggle begins. When these aspects of ourselves emerge it seems "obvious" that they do so because of the other person. After all, the aspects weren't there before the person showed up, were they? People lock into power struggles over whose fault it is or trying to get the other person to change. The struggles sap the creative energy of the relationship and set the stage for dissolution or rigidification. Having helped approximately fifteen hundred couples through this difficult period, we can say with certainty that it is one of the most challenging things you will ever be faced with in life. If this passage in a relationship is negotiated successfully, there is no upper limit on how much love and creativity will be expressed; if not, great pain is often the result. One of our clients was a prisoner of war during the Second World War who was tortured by his captors. When asked to compare that pain to the pain he was experiencing in the wake of his wife's departure, he unhesitatingly said that the pain of the terminated relationship was far worse. "At least I had a way to deal with the pain of physical torture. I could take it, or I could pass out. But this . . . there's's no way out."

All of us can sympathize. We know the difficulty of handling emotional pain. It is complicated by the lack of training any of us gets in how to be in close relationships. Unless you went to a very unusual school, there were no classes on how to solve relationship problems, how to deal with feelings, and how to communicate with the hidden sides of ourselves. But the very nature of emotional pain provides another barrier. With physical pain, there is a clear solution: Remove the stimulus causing the pain. With our emotional lives, the problem is much trickier. Are we victims or volunteers? Much of the pain we experience is due not to the actions of others but on how we see the world.

Pulling out some therapy files at random, we find the following issues that emerged, seemingly from "nowhere," as people got closer in relationships.

- A deep fear of being abandoned
- The fear of being overwhelmed, engulfed
- Rage about childhood violations
- A desire to be taken care of completely by the other person
- Hypersensitivity to criticism

In each of these cases and hundreds more like them, clients swore to us that they did not know the issue was a problem until it popped up in the relationship. None of these issues would cause problems in relationships if we simply said, for example, "Honey, I just became aware that I have a deep fear of abandonment that is coming up now in our relationship. I hereby commit myself to taking full responsibility for clearing it up." Instead, when the issue comes up it looks like the other person has been the vehicle for its entry into our lives. In other words, we tend to project blame onto the other person.

PROJECTION PRODUCES BOTH PAIN AND POSSIBILITY

Here lies the crux of the matter. The major stumbling block in the relationships of the majority of the couples we have counseled has been projection. Projection in this context is when A blames B for something that actually belongs to A. An example: Marjorie blames Bill for flirting with Susie at the party. Bill blames Marjorie for being on his case and trying to tell him what to do. In counseling they find that this problem is rooted in projections on both of their parts. Marjorie and her mother were abandoned by her father when she was a child, resulting in great hardship for her. Based on this experience, she is hypervigilant toward any move Bill might make toward leaving her. She is an abandonment waiting to happen. She sees Bill's conversation with Susie as flirting. Bill's background, having grown up in a military family with an authoritarian father, makes him hypervigilant toward people telling him what he can and cannot do. He is a criticism waiting to happen. When they come in for counseling, they have no idea what the real issues are. They truly think it is the other person's fault. Imagine the relief of finding out what the real problem is! But, like many strong medicines, accepting personal responsibility can be tough to swallow. It is not something that many people know how to do with grace. Especially when it seems so obvious that it is the other person's fault! Many people—even the nicest and most intelligent people—prefer to stay locked in power struggles rather than look into the true source of the struggle within themselves.

Before rushing to judge projection harshly, let us all remember that projection gives us the possibility of change. Without projection, we would have a hard time seeing our hidden selves. The hidden self can be discerned in dreams, in our fantasies, in our body language and verbal language, but to interpret these elements of ourselves requires special skills. However, it takes no training to turn our attention to the repetitive patterns in our close relationships and see our hidden selves come to light. Any pattern that produces dissatisfaction can be seen as a projection from some past event. If we pay attention to those patterns we can readily see the areas of ourselves that require fine-tuning or major overhaul.

This is easier said than done. A great deal of commitment, courage, and practice is required to start viewing all our problems as projections. It is always very tempting to disown responsibility, to point the finger of blame, to claim victimhood. Nature has given us the wonderful gift of awareness, but many of us use it sparingly or unwisely. Every time we repeat a pattern that does not yield satisfaction and closeness in relationships, it is possible to use our awareness to look carefully into the issue. If we approach ourselves with an attitude of humble inquiry, there are great rewards in terms of relationship learning. But all too often we use these opportunities for growth as justifications for holding more tenaciously to our old positions, the positions that do not bring happiness but are simply familiar.

THREE POWERFUL STRATEGIES

We have found that there are three things that people do that entrench them more deeply in the ruts in which they are stuck. Thousands of times in therapy we have seen that problems are caused by not accepting feelings, by not telling the truth, and by not keeping agreements. By turning these three practices into their positive opposites, three very powerful prescriptions for successful relationships come into being. They are:

- Feel all your feelings (and allow others to feel theirs).
- Tell all the truth.
- Keep all your agreements.

The first one is absolutely essential for healthy living in general. When we do not allow ourselves to know and experience our feelings, we are put into conflict with ourselves. When the truth is not acknowledged and spoken, a fundamental disharmony dominates the relationship. Complicating this problem is the fact that human beings are a lot more intuitive and telepathic than we might think. We often know when the truth is not being spoken, but we often avoid confronting these hunches.

This principle has resulted in many amusing incidents for the authors. On the talk show circuit we have become indentified as the couple who advocate absolute honesty in close relationships. The producer of a popular show called our offices one day and said, "These people are the truth doctors, aren't they?" When we first began talking on radio and TV about telling the truth, we were not prepared for the controversies that would arise. It seemed obvious to us that if you tell the truth you have a relationship; if you don't, you don't. A relationship is between two equals who are telling the truth to each other. Anything else is an entanglement, not a relationship. Our first clue came in the early eighties, during one of our first television appearances. We were chatting on about the need for honesty when we noticed that the host, an extremely handsome, suave, and cool guy, had sweat pouring down his face. On the commercial break, he leaned over, mopping his brow, and asked us if we meant that people were supposed to tell the truth about *everything*. It seemed that we had touched a nerve with him.

It has turned out to be a sore spot for society in general. There is currently a backlash against honesty. We have always said that truth is the strongest aphrodisiac, the way to keep the romance flowing in a close love relationship. Recent popular relationship books advocate lying to your partner and not even trying to keep romance alive. The truth is dangerous, say these authors, and as for enduring romance—forget it! Of course, we know that this point of view is absurd, but we can see where it is rooted. There is tremendous fear of the truth in society at large. Some say that lying is the glue that holds the whole operation together. Political analysts have pointed out that the American solution to dissatisfaction with Richard Nixon—when he lied the sweat literally rolled down his face—was to elect a professional actor to play the role of president. Actors are well paid for being able to lie so effectively that we believe it. As Laurence Olivier put it: "It took me a while to figure out that the secret of acting was honesty. Once I learned to fake that, I had it made."

In close relationships we all have to get skilled enough in telling the truth that we see that truth produces greater aliveness. Probably the most common resistance to telling the truth that we hear in therapy is that people are afraid that if they tell the truth their partners will be hurt. When we go deeper into this issue with them, they invariably discover that the real truth is that they do not want to have to put up with the other person's reaction. It seems that many people prefer the deadness of ritualized truthhiding in their relationships to the raw, electric aliveness that telling the truth produces.

One way to keep a relationship in stasis or in uproar is to break agreements. Many people use this as their main strategy for relationship misery. It took the authors a lot of looking to see that not keeping agreements destroyed the potential for creativity. In our own relationship, we found that underneath many upsets with each other was some agreement that had been forgotten. As we began to pay attention to this problem in ourselves, we began to see how prevalent this problem was in our clients. One of our clients with a closed head injury actually traced her accident to a broken agreement. She had agreed not to spend time with a former lover, an agreement she had made with her partner but did not feel committed to keep. She sneaked out of the house one evening, spent time with the lover, and was hurrying back home. She was preoccupied with rehearsing various strategies for lying about where she had been when she rear-ended another car that she simply did not see. Looking carefully at this situation, we can see why she might be an accident waiting to happen. Her consciousness was divided in two: not here, not there. Part of her was at home, trying to explain a situation without actually telling the truth. Part of her was trying to drive a car. There was not enough of her available to do the job at hand. How many accidents come from just this sort of division?

The three fundamental requirements of close relationships—experiencing feelings, telling the truth, keeping agreements—are ways of staying in unity with ourselves and others. When we shut off our feelings, we divide ourselves in half. When we do not tell the truth, we divide ourselves from others. So it is with failing to keep agreements. Some part of us and others is always keeping track of the agreements we have made and the agreements others have made with us. When those are not kept, we have to confront the broken agreements or shut them out of our awareness. Confronting our own broken agreements and those others have broken is scary. It is not a popular choice, nor easily done. It is much more likely that we will swallow the confrontation, preferring to avoid the possible unpleasantness. But this is a troublesome move, guaranteed to put us out of harmony at a fundamental level.

In our therapy practices, we work quite a bit with people who are in chronic pain or who have longstanding physical problems of psychological origin. In the case of headaches, for example, the person often has a history of swallowing important communications, such as anger. The boss will make a demand, the employee will feel angry about it but will not say anything, only to go home from work early because of a headache. How many million hours of lost productivity each year are the result of just this sort of misplaced communication? We have shown hundreds of people how to clear pain out of their bodies by communicating the truth of their feelings in nonthreatening ways.

There is an old saying: The truth will out. If the truth of our feelings and deeds is told, a healthy relationship is possible. If the truth is withheld, it will eventually find some way out into the light. Even after many years of choosing the truth, we are still faced with the choice every day. We find in our personal relationship that there is always something new we are learning about ourselves—we are continually finding a new edge—and that a continued recommitment to the truth is necessary. Now, at midlife, both of us are discovering many layers of ourselves that we buried long ago in order to survive in our early family life. For example, Kathlyn left behind her creative side at an early age in order to be Mother's helper. She had to grow up quickly at the age of nine, when her mother became ill. This event was not good or bad: it simply was. Her new role took on a life of its own, and she adopted a persona that she now calls Supercompetent.

We all slip into personas, just as we slip into a raincoat on a stormy day. It protects us from the elements, but it is not essentially who we are. Kathlyn's Supercompetent persona concealed a creative artist. Now the Supercompetent aspect of herself, though very successful, is no longer satisfying to her. In other words, she wants greater freedom of expression. She wants to give energy to parts of her other than the reliable hard-worker. Herein lies a major problem for many people. Some of us are able to shed a persona gracefully when it is no longer working. Others of us wrestle with our persona raincoats as we try to remove them. Or, just as likely, others wrestle with us, trying to keep them on. Family and friends can get just as attached to our personas as we do.

One of the big messages life brings us is: Be yourself. As life proceeds, and especially as we get into our thirties and forties, we get strong hints from the world around us that it is essential to uncover who we really are. If we remove our masks successfully, we are able to uncover parts of ourselves that we can draw on for the energy to fuel the second half of our lives. If we do not, we are likely to circulate through the same personas long after they are tired and worn out. Certainly this problem is visible to us as therapists every day. People come in, stuck in personas they have been wearing for too long. It is often extraordinarily difficult to get them to try out a new way of being. Often we have marveled: Why would we humans become so comfortable with, attached to, and afraid of giving up something that is producing so much unhappiness?

To find the answer to this crucial question, we need to look at how the personality is built.

WHERE OUR PERSONALITIES COME FROM

As people work on themselves—through the self-inquiry of therapy and other procedures—they become aware of an aspect of themselves that is frequently lost in childhood. The word we use for this aspect is *essence,* the part of us all that is free, clear, and uncluttered with the learning processes of life. Essence simply *is:* It is pure consciousness, with nothing added. When in touch with essence, human beings may have feelings, for example, but the feelings do not overwhelm them. Similarly, we may wear personas, but if we are in touch with essence, we wear them lightly. When out of touch with essence, our personas overshadow us, leading us to become attached to them.

Personas may then develop a life of their own. They work. At a certain stage of development, they may be our only choice. As we use them over and over again, finding that we can get some of our needs met by these false selves, we gradually forget that they are not really us. We mistake them for our true selves, only to wake up later in life wondering: Who am I? Where did I go? How did I lose touch with the part of me that is real? These questions can serve as the stimulus for our return to essence, but sometimes they are never asked or encouraged. All too many people go to their graves without answering the fundamental questions of their existence. They settle for the small pleasures of life—the search for the ultimate cocktail, dessert, or sitcom—rather than becoming the agents of their own destinies.

In our travels we have been surprised to find that this lack of self-knowledge is often greater in affluent societies. One would think that citizens of the Third World would be too caught up in the struggle for food and shelter to ask the bigger philosophical questions. But the exact opposite seems to be true. On a train in India, for example, practically anyone—traveling salesman, pauper, sweeper—will be happy to engage in a dialogue about the subtleties of human existence. It is much more unlikely to strike up such a conversation on a Swiss train or a New York subway. In fact, simple eye contact is often avoided in such settings.

When we have strong feelings—fear, anger, grief—our essence is often overshadowed throughout the duration of the feelings. If we develop an effective method of clearing feelings from our bodies and minds, we can then return to essence. When essence is strong, we know that while we may have feelings, we are larger than they are. When essence is overwhelmed, our feelings seem larger than we are. In growing up there is little useful information available about how to clear ourselves of feelings. If we had a guardian angel, when we are grieving, for example, our angel might say, "Let yourself feel the sadness deeply. Don't resist it. Contact it in your body. Breathe deeply with it. Communicate it clearly to someone who'll listen nonjudgmentally." Unfortunately, guardian angels are in short supply, and society seems too often to teach us the exact opposite behavior.

We tell our clients who are immersed in feeling: Don't flee or fight—*flow*. In other words, tune in to feelings and be with them until they pass. Feelings are like thunderstorms, with a beginning, a middle, and an end. Unless impeded, they will move through, even cleansing the air. However, the antifeeling messages of society cause many problems. By teaching us to withhold feelings from ourselves, and especially by teaching us to conceal them from each other, we set the stage for relationships built on concealment rather than revealment.

This problem brings us to the next element on which personalities are built. If we are out of touch with essence and the feelings that obscure essence, we need to come up with strategies to relate to people around us. In other words, if we find that being real does not work very well, we need to come up with something that does. These strategies, which we call personas, are the masks we learn to wear to get our needs met. As we work with clients we find that they learned to wear many such masks, because there are many people and situations that may require different faces as we grow up. It would be ideal, perhaps, if people saw our essences as we grew up. If they saw who we really were, and went about the task of nurturing our essences, then we might not need to put on false faces to get recognition. But in the real world of family interaction, we are often split into many parts. We may learn to adopt a Supercompetent persona with one parent and a Victim persona with another. On another day we may find that getting a sore throat works to avoid some responsibility, so we begin to use a Get Sick persona at various stressful times in life.

Some personas are highly rewarded, others are frowned upon

by society. A person may cling to his Delinquent/Rebel persona for a lifetime, even though it has brought nothing but misery to him. Why would he cling to such a persona? A persona is not simply there to get external rewards, it serves a complex inner function and stays in place by a certain way in which we use it in social relations. Personas are used to control feelings; while they are in place we do not have to confront the often stormy or deadly feelings on which they are based. We often gravitate to a particular persona at a time in our lives when we have an awesome amount of inner rage, fear, or grief and no way to express it effectively.

Personas are also used as ways of being right and making other people wrong. When in the grip of a persona such as Rebel, it is quite likely that we will band together with fellow Rebels, forming a club based on a shared perception that we are right and *they* are wrong. Then, regardless of what happens to us on the outside—judge, jail, or junkiedom—we are able to preserve a sense of self, albeit one founded on a false and costly view of who we are. We become willing to trade happiness, peace of mind, and success for being right.

Nowhere is this phenomenon more apparent than in the counseling of couples. People come in who have not drawn a happy breath in their relationships in years. Upon exploration, they find that the whole time they have been choosing to remain in personas that do not work, simply to be right and to make someone else wrong. Being right and making wrong is best thought of as an addiction. We notice that when people give up this habit it frequently brings on something that looks very much like withdrawal symptoms, sometimes including physical symptoms. For example, we pointed out to a couple a deeply ingrained tendency to make each other wrong. This tendency was so habitual that it had never occurred to either of them that the "make wrong" was going on entirely in their respective minds. When we pointed out that there was nothing intrinsically "wrong" with either one of them, they looked at us with mouths agape. We encouraged them to begin to focus on their respective minds as the culprit, seeing their wrong-making machinery as the problem rather than the other person.

We got a call two days later from one of them, who said, "I don't know what to do now that I'm not criticizing [the mate]. What am I going to do with all my time?" We suggested that they turn their attention to finding out how they could enjoy life and how they could produce something creative for the world. This problem is the same one faced by many recovering addicts. The addiction structured their time and their lives. Without it, how would the time be filled? Some make the happy discovery that the same amount of time and energy formerly wasted on the addiction can be turned into productive actions. Others do not get their free energy channeled in a satisfying way that yields creative results.

PROJECTION AND PERSONAS

Projections flow from our personas. Once we lock into a particular persona the world—and the people in it—look different. For example, Dependent/Clingy people see others as those to whom they can cling or those to whom they cannot. A Ramblin' Man—fearing commitment and engulfment—sees people as those who will give him space or those who will not. One person comes into a party and sees people being phony. We see what we believe, not what is actually there. Granted, there are times when we see what's really there, but the wise person will first consider that everything he or she sees is a projection.

The problem of projection needs to be mastered if close relationships are to be successful. What is the best way to find out what your projections are? The technique is simple but maddening at times: Just look at what you most complain about in others and apply it to yourself. Gay, for example, complained constantly about the anger that a former relationship partner beamed at him: "My programming led me to suffer in silence. Her programming led her to suffer loudly, operatically. Pretty much from the day we met the focus of her anger became me. According to her, her life had been unblemished until I entered. Oddly enough, I maintained the same thing. Friends would ask me why I just didn't walk away. I couldn't tell them why at the time, but now it's clear to me that

I needed to learn about a key projection in my life. Specifically, I had disowned my anger, holding it inside. I buried it under tension and overeating. In the relationship I stuffed myself constantly, and when it ended I lost a hundred pounds in a year. Finally one day I woke up to what is now painfully obvious: What I most complained about in her was what I most needed to learn about in myself. I needed to learn about anger, how to feel and how to express it. As long as it was so deeply bottled up in myself, I needed to see it dramatically in others. How else could I learn about it? The relationship effectively ended one magic day when I stopped pointing the finger at her and brought it back around to aim at myself. I asked: What is it about me that keeps creating this situation? It was painful to look at, but what I got was that I was angry myself. I quit thinking that our relationship problem was her anger and instead took on the project of working on my own angry feelings."

Facing the projection issue is one of the most courageous acts anyone can ever make. It is so tempting to blame and justify. The august U.S. Senate, in the wake of the Clarence Thomas affair, went to the trouble of appointing a special person to find out who leaked the story! Many concerned citizens probably wondered why the senators did not put a special consultant onto the problem of how to reveal the truth rather than conceal it. We have watched many couples in therapy struggle with this issue. Almost everyone comes in with an agenda of blame and projection. Each person is pretty well convinced that it actually is the other person's fault. Each of them must loosen the grip on this projection to solve the problems in the relationship. Each must abandon the pointing finger and look inside. The moment we ask the question: What is it within me that is contributing to this problem? the projection loses its stranglehold on us. The alternative question: Why is this other person (and the world) doing this to me? puts us in an unequal victim position to all of life.

TAKING RESPONSIBILITY

The corollary of dropping projection is taking full responsibility. But it must be a certain type of responsibility. It cannot be a definition of responsibility that involves blame in any way. Some people think of responsibility in terms of "Who's to blame here?" Assigning blame is based on a very primitive understanding of responsibility, but it is an association that is often impressed on our minds due to childhood traumas. After all, when we break the cookie jar while stealing cookies, we often hear "Who's responsible for this?" in a blame context. Admission of responsibility is followed by punishment.

If responsibility does not involve blame, what is it? What is an understanding that serves us in close relationships? In a phrase: Responsibility is a celebration of wholeness. In order to claim responsibility we must open up to every hidden part of ourselves and look within to find out how we are creating the situation we are in. A relationship is between two or more people who are 100 percent responsible for their lives; anything else is an entanglement. Note that we have not said that you need to take 110 percent or 152 percent responsibility. In couples therapy, we urge people to let the other person have room to take 100 percent. We have worked with many people who took too much responsibility. They were martyrs who did not demand that others be responsible. An extreme example is the depressed middle-aged woman who rode a bus across town each week to deliver her thirty-six-year-old son's ironing to him because she didn't want to trouble him to come get it. For years she had wanted to ask him to pick up his laundry, but she was afraid he would be upset. If your life is based on such a cockeyed set of assumptions, depression is nearly assured.

Nor will 99 percent responsibility do. Any time we are coming into a situation with less than 100 percent responsibility we are requiring someone else to pick up the slack. It is possible to take responsibility even in extreme circumstances. For inspiration we sometimes read the books of Viktor Frankl. Frankl was incarcerated in a Nazi concentration camp during World War II. Most of us would agree that this is a situation in which one could rightfully claim victimhood. But he did not stop there. He decided to take responsibility for being happy and creative even in such adverse conditions. And he did so, turning his experience into a remarkable journey of growth and service. Later he went on to become one of the most distinguished therapists of our time.

A healthy relationship is one in which both people are absolutely committed to their own wholeness. They realize that an entanglement occurs when one person or the other avoids full responsibility. The potential for creativity is enormous in a relationship. The potential for destructiveness is enormous in an entanglement. M. Scott Peck, in his widely read book *The Road Less Traveled,* puts it very succinctly: Mental health problems are basically disturbances of responsibility. Neurotics take too much; people with character disorders take too little. We would go further to say that almost all of us take the wrong kind of responsibility. As human beings, we tend to understand responsibility as a burden, or we see it as a restriction of our freedom.

AN EXAMPLE OF A CHOICE FOR ALIVENESS

What we often do not see is that true responsibility is the path to greatest aliveness. When we can celebrate the awareness—I had a role creating all this!—we have the greatest possible space for growth. Accepting full responsibility for the way our lives go also gives us the most power to change any aspect of life we do not like. We saw a beautiful example of this issue not long ago in therapy. A couple came in at the point of splitting up. They agreed to three sessions of therapy to find out if they could salvage the relationship. At first, neither would take any responsibility for the way the relationship was going. They could only agree on one thing: It was, without question, the other person's fault. For her, his inability to speak the truth, particularly about his feelings, was at the root of the problem. Also, she was sick of his lack of responsibility. For him, the relationship was a disaster because of her endless criticism. It took a whole session just to get them each thoroughly ventilated. We did not attempt to do much besides listen to their complaints about each other.

But at the beginning of the second session we popped a big question to them. Would they be willing to do whatever was necessary *in themselves* to heal the relationship? After some deliberation, they said yes. This agreement gave us the freedom to ask a deeper question. To him we said, "Would you be willing to find out your role in perpetuating your wife's critical strategy?" To her we said, "Would you be willing to discover your role in your husband's difficulty in speaking the truth of his feelings and in being responsible?" Both exploded into a rage of denial, vehemently maintaining that they had nothing to do with each other's issues. We rode out this eruption, then firmly reminded them that they had agreed to look at their own roles in perpetuating the problems in the relationship. Slowly they reined themselves in and began to focus inward. For the first time, they began seriously to entertain the possibility of true responsibility.

She broke through first. Could it be, she mused, that she had some role in his difficulty expressing feelings? We quickly put this insight to the test. We asked her to listen to him expressing a feeling. We asked them to face each other. Tell her something you're scared about, we said to him. He closed his eyes for a moment. "I'm scared you might leave me." A split second later she howled sarcastically. "Oh, sure. Like I'm really going to walk out and move into some dinky little studio apartment and leave you sitting in a $250,000 house that I've spent the last ten years decorating." She went on in this vein for another thirty seconds or so.

When she came to a halt, we pointed out that no one in their right mind would tell the truth about his feelings if he got that kind of reaction. Of course he would keep them bottled up, even if there were no other reasons to do so. Her jaw literally dropped. We went further. When did this critical part of you come into being? She told us a story of a perfectionist upbringing, where she was criticized seemingly on a minute-by-minute basis. We turned to him. How is it inevitable, given your learning history, that you would invite someone into your life who criticizes you a lot? His past involved a critical mother and a sloppy father. His growing up was fraught with their battle, until they split up in his early teens.

The couple's relationship began to heal when they quit pointing the finger of blame. They took the same energy that was being eaten up by accusation and used it for exploration of themselves. By the end of their third session they were excited about using their relationship as an arena for self-discovery.

THE ART OF INTIMACY

Our whole approach to relationship therapy grew out of inventing our own relationship. Most of us have too many models for poor relationships. Few of us have an abundance of healthy models. When we got together in 1980, we looked around us for models on which to base our relationship. We did not find any. We were very clear about what we didn't want. But where to look for heroes? Not finding any gave us impetus to design what we wanted from scratch. The first thing we did was to sit down after dinner one evening and come up with a list of the things on which a healthy relationship could thrive. Now, well over a decade later, this list has grown considerably. Based on our current state of evolution, here is what we think constitutes a good relationship.

- Both people are totally committed to employing the relationship as the arena for self-knowledge.
- Both people are committed to being close.
- Both people are committed to their own ultimate individual development.
- Both people tell all the truth, all the time. Anything else is an entanglement. No exceptions.
- Both people take full responsibility for themselves. There are no victims and no villains.
- Conflicts are resolved in a win/win manner. No one has to lose in order for someone else to win.
- Both people consistently demonstrate that they choose hav-

ing a good time over being right and making the other person wrong.

As we have watched couples switch over to living this new way, we have marveled at how powerful such simple things can be. On the surface each of these points looks easy, yet each involves lifetime commitments. Frequently couples come up to us at workshops to tell us that they have been working for two years on learning to tell each other the truth or communicate what they want to each other. Sometimes the simplest things can be the hardest to learn. But they are often the most powerfully transformative learnings. We have seen cancer go into remission when the person learned how to speak the truth. We have seen a cold and sore throat disappear within an hour when the person said "I forgive you" to his partner. We have seen thousands of people who have made the choice to move toward health and happiness in their relationships. It is deeply moving to us to see how quickly people can progress when they have an outline of the goals they are seeking. After all, it only took humans a hundred years to go from locomotive to moon rocket. The speed at which people are moving to transform their relationships has given us, as therapists, authors, and fellow-inhabitants of the planet, a great deal of inspiration to continue the work.

CHAPTER TWO

Love in Action: A Couple Transforms Their Relationship

....

Every summer we host a training program for therapists, held at a retreat center in the Rockies. It is always one of the highs of the year for us; we get to introduce a new group of enthusiastic learners to the principles of relationship described in these pages. And we get to do it on our home turf, in the majestic mountains that have been our home for nearly two decades. One of the teaching tools we use is to demonstrate the relationship principles in "live" sessions. The transcript you are about to read comes from one of those training sessions. A married couple, both therapists, volunteered to work on a deeply troubling issue in front of the group. Given the content of the sessions, their courage in baring these issues to the group is to be especially applauded.

The session demonstrates quite eloquently how powerful these ideas can be. Other than trimming out some "uhs" and repetitions, we have not edited the material. It appears just as it happened.

Italic letters will be used to indicate when either Kathlyn or Gay is speaking. The setting is a conference room overlooking a valley surrounded by high mountain peaks. Beth and Don are seated in two chairs facing each other in the center of a circle of about thirty-five people. Gay and Kathlyn also are seated in the center, forming a square with Beth and Don. The session will last a little over an hour.

What are the issues you would like to work on?

Don: We've been married twenty years. Beth recently had an affair. She wants to remain friends with him. It's difficult to deal with open-endedness. I want to continue our marriage, and I feel threatened with her having—I have a lot of feelings . . . Wanting her back hurts.

Beth: Don has made it clear what he wants. I'm not sure what I want.

Given all of that, would you be willing to clear up this issue in our time together today?

Don: Yes.

Beth: Yes.

Go back, Beth, to the moment you began the other relationship; what exactly happened?

Beth: I haven't ever given myself permission to pursue what I really want . . . so I did, with this man. I feel like I've been trapped all my life—and I didn't want to spend my whole life that way. So I just . . . acted on impulse . . . did what I wanted.

And does that relationship—the way it feels—remind you of anything?

Beth: My first date in high school. He seemed a lot like my dad, too, as time went on. I don't know . . . I don't know . . .

I notice you say "I don't know" quite a bit. Say "I don't know" a few times and see what feelings come up.

Beth: I don't know . . . I don't know. I guess I really want both men, and when I talk about it I get scared. I'm afraid to say.

So you go to "I don't know" to avoid having to be with the fear.
Beth: [*Nods*]

When you say you're afraid to tell the truth, is the fear that you will be judged wrong?
Beth: I withhold the truth to keep from the pain. I'm afraid I'll hurt him.

Don, would you rather hear the truth rather than keep the relationship? Can you choose the truth, or do you want to keep the relationship so much you don't want to hear the truth?
Don: I want to hear the truth.

Beth, how do you feel? Which one would you go to when the chips are down?
Beth: I don't know.
Don: She's been telling the truth about her feelings for him, and now I feel like it's a weapon and I'm going to get nailed with it.

Is there a way in which all of this is inevitable? Do you remember, Don, the moment you found out about all of this?
Don: It was the worst thing possible. It was a shock, but it was also a relief. Because I [already] felt something was wrong.

Check carefully in yourselves. Is there a way in which these feelings are familiar to you? Are there other incidents with these qualities?
Don: Yeah. The other time she had an affair. My thought was, "To heck with it, I'll just go my own way."

Is there a theme here? In this relationship Beth is the Bad Guy and the Wild One, and Don gets to be the Victim and the Cautious One.
Beth: I feel pushed to be the fire in our relationship.
Don: I thought if I was good enough this wouldn't happen again.

Let's look at how all this might be inevitable, given your ways of being. Beth, what to you believe you have to be in order to be with Don? What does he require of you?
Beth: I'm supposed to be exciting and sexy and attractive and wild.

How about you, Don? What does Beth require of you?
Don: That I'm reliable, good—a provider and caretaker.

And, Beth, how do you make Don wrong?
Beth: That he's a couch potato; he's uninterested in the kids.

Don, what did you think of her about two minutes after you found out about this?
Don: That she was compulsive, dramatic, bad, mean, uncaring. How could she do this to me?

Beth, what were you feeling?
Beth: It had nothing to do with him.
Don: She wasn't going to tell me—to protect me—and then she goes and tells three of my friends.

So, Beth, you accepted the role of Bad Guy. You provide the fire, and, Don, you accepted the steady role. Those two roles aren't working anymore. Would you be willing to resolve all this in a way that doesn't make anybody right or wrong? Would you be willing to be each other's allies in your evolution and to create a positive future today, right now?
Don: Yes.
Beth: Yes.

It looks like you're both addicted to these two roles—the Wild One and the Victim. Let's look at where those two roles came from.
Don: I can see where I got my role. My dad was a total victim, and he was always right. I do the same thing. I use this victim thing as my way of being right and making Beth wrong.
Beth: I'm not sure. My mother's main role was to play stupid. I

guess my Wild One role is a way to get people to wake up. See Me! Look at me! I exist!

So [each] take a moment to love yourself for adopting those roles. Give yourself some loving acceptance for using those acts. But, also tune in to how those roles are not really you.

Don: So you're saying that we're just playing out a drama between two old survival roles we adopted in our childhoods.

Right. And these roles are about four-year-olds. The possibility exists now for you to design how you want your relationship to be as grown-ups.

Beth: [*Takes a deep breath*] Wow. That's an interesting idea! [*Everybody laughs*]

Another thing to look at. Are you playing out each other's hidden opposite?

Beth: What do you mean?

Well, maybe Don has a secret Rebel hidden underneath that burdened Victim role. And, Beth, maybe you have a secret Victim buried under your Rebel.

Don: So that I would require Beth to act out my Rebel, because I've got it too buried to be in touch with it. I somehow require that she wake me up.

Because?

Don: Because, I guess, I have trouble waking myself up.

Beth: He has three alarm clocks, no kidding!

So you require a lot of outside stimulation to wake you up.

Don: Yeah.

So, Don, would you be willing to become your own alarm clock, so you don't require Beth to wake you up in ways you find obnoxious?

Don: Whew. I guess.

Is that a yes or a no?
Don: [*Laughs and takes a big breath*] Okay. Yes. That's what I want.

Let's see how it would work with you, Beth.
Beth: Okay.

Maybe underneath your Wild One act you have a deep need for grounding, to stay balanced and centered. You don't provide that for yourself, so you require Don to play a couch potato and a cop, an anchor to keep you from messing up too much.
Beth: But then I rebel against it. I act out in ways that are hurtful to Don and the kids.

Would you be willing to find a balance? A way to be wild and creative in a totally positive way?
Beth: Yes, definitely.

Check inside yourselves. Are you both willing to be completely whole, in a way that's completely safe for both of you?
Beth: Yes.
Don: Yes.

Move a little closer and hold hands. Would you be willing to tell each other the truth?
Both: Yes.

Go ahead. Each of you say things that are true, which cannot be argued about. We'll give you some coaching.
Don: I feel taken advantage of.
Beth: I feel like I let you take advantage of me.

Okay, both these things could be argued about. Go to a deeper level. What's the real truth underneath that.
Beth: I'm confused. I'm angry at men. Men in general.

Do you remember the moment you made that decision?
Beth: It was early, before I went to school. I hated seeing my

mother do all the work while my father and my brothers just ran around. I hated having to help her all the time.

And what's the truth for you, Don?
Don: I don't feel appreciated.

Go even deeper. Get underneath all the victim stuff.
Don: I'm scared. I'm helpless. Dependent.

What time in life does this remind you of?
Don: It's exactly like when my parents split up and I went to live with my grandparents.

So when Beth gets interested in another man, your abandonment fears are triggered.
Don: Yeah.

Take a moment to love yourself for those feelings. Love them like you love your kids.
Don: [*Crying*]

Do you both want this marriage?
Don: Yes.
Beth: Yes.

Do you love each other?
Beth: Yes.
Don: Yes.

Okay. We'd like you to set aside ten minutes a day for homework. Would you do that?
Both: Yes.

Take ten minutes and sit down, hand in hand, just like you are right now. Make eye contact and tell each other the truth. Stay connected and get underneath all the stuff that can be argued about. Tell the truth that can't possibly be argued about. Okay?

Both: Okay.

Outcome: The workshop concluded the next day, and we did not see Don and Beth again for a month, until a trip to Colorado made it possible for them to have another meeting with us in Colorado Springs. Following that, we had a joint telephone session with them when they called from their home in the Midwest. We continued to work with the same themes they identified in the session presented above. Rather quickly, Beth's relationship with the other man dissolved. No dramatic exercise of willpower was required; she just lost interest. She was surprised at how the intensity of feelings for him, which had seemed so compelling, could fade so quickly. Our hunch was that as soon as she saw that the feelings were an outgrowth of her Rebel and Alarm Clock roles, she had no further use for them. As soon as Don got out from under his Victim role and began to be his own alarm clock, he had no need for Beth to be the Wild One.

When we last heard from them, they were happier than ever before, busy with the task of designing a relationship based on what they now consciously want.

In presenting a case which has such a positive outcome, it is tempting to think that what Beth and Don accomplished is easy. It is not, of course. What is required is commitment and a willingness to explore, to sail off into the unknown. Sometimes the courage that couples show reminds us of explorers like Columbus and Balboa, who went off toward the horizon with little to go on but their commitment. In this case, Beth and Don had the necessary prerequisites for turning the adventure of relationship into a successful journey: They were both committed to the relationship and to learning about themselves. By the power of these commitments they were able to transform a potential breakdown and breakup into a breakthrough.

CHAPTER THREE

Our Story: How Our Own Relationship Developed

•••••••

Our own relationship has been the main beneficiary of all the ideas and practices we are describing in this book. Our life together has given us all the psychological growth, spritual evolution, love, and material rewards that we could ever have dreamed of. We have managed to create together a family and a career that is so different from and so much better than anything we saw around us growing up that we are frequently amazed at how it all came about. Actually, what seems like magic is almost always the result of tiny moments of choice—decisions for growth rather than for stagnation. We have made thousands of choices along the way that have contributed to the success of our relationship. In this chapter we would like to share some of our own personal lives and our choicepoints, focusing particularly on how we generated our relationship and formed the ideas in the book.

We met in January 1980, just a few days into the new decade. We will speak in our own individual voices for a moment, then switch back to *we*. Gay was in an unusual state of serenity and turmoil, having just decided the month before to leave the relationship he was in. In his words: "It was a stormy time, but at the center of myself I felt a rare sense of peace. I had come to a resolution point and had made a decision that I felt would change all of my life. I didn't know how it would all work out, of course, but I knew the change would be profound.

"In late 1979, I had found myself in an escalating series of quarrels with the woman with whom I had shared my life for the past five years. The quarrels had a familiar theme. Usually they would go like this: She would get upset about my talking to another woman at a party or some other social gathering. I had been sexually monogamous with her, and I would get enraged at being falsely accused. I would rail against her trying to control me. You're trying to limit my freedom! I can't breathe if I'm fenced in! We would both become self-righteous about our positions, digging in our heels and refusing to budge. I would get extremely upset at her unwillingness to look at what this issue might be about in herself. I knew that it was an old pattern in her life that she had played out in other relationships, and I also knew that her father had committed numerous infidelities that had eventually contributed to her parents' divorce. I would retreat to my little cabin on the back of our property and meditate/sulk for three days. These were almost always three-day episodes—and in general they happened about once a month. But in that fall of 1979 they became more frequent than they had been, off and on, since the relationship began in late 1974.

"The event that changed everything took place in early December 1979. I came back from being at a party held by some of my graduate students. Having gotten lost in an animated conversation at the party—of course surrounded by intelligent and attractive women!—I came home later than I had predicted. Confronted about this broken agreement, I mentioned that I had gotten so caught up in the discussion that I had forgotten the time. I went on further to do something that I had rarely if ever done: I told the detailed truth about the party, the people who were there, and the specific people with whom I had talked. I had become accustomed to giving carefully edited versions of my social activities, to save myself from the fury of her reactions. But this time I decided to tell the whole truth. Predictably, much uproar unsued. During this heated discussion, I had a moment of supreme clarity. I realized I was repeating the same theme I had been repeating for years. As my programmed self continued the argument on autopilot, another part of me asked several life-changing questions: What if this were not completely her fault? What if this had something to do with me? What was it about me that made this pattern inevitable? You may laugh that it took a therapist so long to consider this possibility, since I spend half my days asking people to look at this very issue. At any rate, I asked another question: Was there something I needed to learn about myself that, if I learned it, would enable me to transcend this pattern? I stopped talking right in the midst of the argument and stood stock still in the center of the floor. I was later told that my jaw dropped open and I had a radiantly awestruck look on my face. I suddenly saw the whole pattern: I had played the same role with my mother from my first days. I would feel smothered by her half the time and abandoned the other half. My mother worked full time, and I was cared for by my grandmother. My mother would rush in at lunch, give me some fast and furious attention (accent on the furious), and then dash back to work. After work the sequence would be repeated. I think she felt so guilty about the arrangement that she felt obligated to parent me in these twenty-minute bursts, even though I might not have needed it at the time.

"The result of all this seemed to be that I developed a huge fear of being engulfed. My belief was that if I got close to someone I would lose my center, my self. So if I got close, I would get scared of being engulfed, then I would do something obnoxious to drive her back. Of course, all this would take place totally unconsciously: To me it just looked like she was on my case and trying to control me by denying me my freedom. Naturally, I had been playing out this script so long that I even had my cheering section, a support group of fellow-mavericks who all agreed that—yes, indeed—she was trying to control me and limit my freedom.

She had her cheering section who agreed that I was the Bad Guy, an incorrigible Ramblin' Man who would quickly revert to the savage state if she took her eye off me. So we were both skilled at making ourselves right. But we were both wrong—dead wrong.

"I stepped out of my persona that day in 1979. In a dizzyingly fast chain of thoughts, I saw the pattern and decided to change it. I chose in that moment to drop it permanently. The pain was too great to continue it. I didn't know what the payoff would be, but I knew one thing for sure: I would rather be alone than replay the pattern one more time. Ever.

"I stopped in the middle of the argument and told my partner what I had just seen. I took full responsibility for the pattern and did my best to describe the source of the programming in my relationship with my mother. I asked her if she was interested in clearing up whatever her end of the pattern was, so that we could find out what our relationship could be outside this script. She said no. She said that it was completely my fault, that she had nothing to do with it, and that we could only have a relationship if I admitted that I was the problem. Okay, I said, I'm the problem. Are you interested in having a relationship in which we both take 100 percent responsibility 100 percent of the time? She thought for a moment, then shocked me with her answer. It was no. She explained lucidly that she was afraid to look into this pattern in herself and that she would rather sacrifice the relationship than open up to it. I was stunned by this decision, but in another way I felt an incredible sense of serenity. I knew I had made a decision that would free me, and I was willing to stick by it. I retreated to my cabin and began to deal with the grief of ending a close relationship, but at a deeper level than the grief I felt a centeredness at the core of myself. Over the next month, I put my attention on figuring out what I wanted in a close relationship. I had been so busy focusing on what I didn't want that I had forgotten to think positively about what the healthy alternatives might be.

"I decided that what I most wanted was a relationship that was not about power struggles, one that celebrated rather than avoided personal responsibility. I never again wanted to fight about whose fault it was. If conflict arose, we would look inside ourselves for the source, not point the finger at the other person. I wanted someone I could work with and play with in complete harmony. I wanted someone who was so committed to her own creativity that both of us would be more creative in the relationship than we were on our own. I really wanted a totally committed spiritual partner for the journey. During the next month I felt a sense of aliveness that had been missing from my life for a while. In early January I flew off to California to teach a workshop at a graduate school. I had taught many workshops at this school, an innovative place where students from twenty-five to seventy-five years old studied transpersonal psychology. As I gathered with the group for the first time, and we formed a large circle, my attention was drawn to one of the doctoral students in the group of perhaps fifty who were in attendance. She was a woman in her early thirties, quite beautiful in the physical sense. But what I most noticed was the radiant glow about her. She looked like a combination of Earth Mother and Angel. I noticed also that she thought all my jokes were uproariously funny. My sense of humor is an acquired taste, based as it is on obscure references and a skewed view of the world. So I am always interested in those people who find it amusing. They are usually in the minority in most groups, but they are always a fascinating minority. During a break, I struck up a conversation with her. I had decided to be unflinchingly honest in all my relationships, so I held nothing back in my communications with her from the very beginning. I saw by her name tag that her name was Kathlyn.

" 'Hello', I said, 'I'd like to spend some time with you. You have a very pure glow about you, and I'm very attracted to you. Would you spend some time with me?' She was taken aback somewhat by the directness of this communication, but she quickly rose to the occasion. She agreed and offered to go get us a couple of sandwiches at lunch break so I could do some further workshop preparation. During lunch, I poured out the whole story of where I was in my life and my relationship. It was important to me to have no artifice with her, nothing held back. As it turned out, the complete candor of our early communications set a tone of honesty in the relationship that has never wavered."

• • •

And now Kathlyn explains, in her own words, what was going on in her life and relationships at the moment we met: "I had also been in a relationship for five years when Gay and I met. The moment I met Gay was a moment of recognition: I realized that another person saw the world in the same way I always had. I had learned to disguise this way of seeing the world, out of a long history of being misunderstood, but I secretly hoped that I would eventually meet someone who shared my worldview.

"I developed what I now call my Chameleon persona very early in life, to adapt to the changing circumstances when my family moved (interestingly, about every five years) with my father's GM job. I learned to observe what was going on by studying people's nonverbal communication. I didn't use those words then, but I see now that I learned systems analysis very early. Being the outsider, frequently in a new city, I learned to observe closely before acting. I remember one humiliating experience of coming into a California school wearing the Oxfords and pleated skirt that was the required uniform in the midwestern school I had just left. It seemed to me that people lived in secret worlds behind elaborate masks, and I was fascinated with what was *really* going on in family, school, and social situations.

"I was involved in a relationship that looked as if it was working well. We had some conflict over the presence of my young son from a previous marriage, but we had rich discussions about inner life, literature, and music. It was really the masterpiece of my Supercompetent persona. I cooked wonderful meals, decorated the house beautifully, always dressed with an eye to pleasing my mate, carried on my private movement therapy practice, and parented. I was Superwoman, carrying out a juggling act that I'm sure many women find familiar.

"At the same time, I felt unaccountably restless and would criticize myself for wanting something more; there was some indefinable thing in my core that would never shut up. It seems clear now that I had essentially decided to go it alone and maintain the guise of the well-adjusted woman. My deepest hungers had always been for truth and meaning, the direct experience of life. I had even developed a profession—movement therapy—to study the meaning hidden behind people's words. Books, movies, meditation, and long walks provided some nourishment, but I hadn't imagined that relationship could be a source of enlightenment. What I had observed in my family and friends' families was a life of rules, roles, and rituals. It was important to look good. I come from a family where three out of five are engineers. I turned that interest in taking things apart to see how they work toward humans, and I found it an endlessly fascinating, if somewhat solitary, occupation.

"But I was essentially split and living in an uncomfortable, unconscious disharmony with myself as a result. Creating the perfect dinner party didn't fix it. Eating secretly in my car didn't heal that split, nor, remarkably, did great sex, which was one anchor of my relationship. I was most interested in the frontiers, in what hadn't been created yet, and when I met Gay, the frontier became reality.

"Several transformations occurred in the moment Gay and I recognized each other. As he was looking around the circle at the first meeting of the workshop, it may have seemed that he was assessing the group's ages, interest level, etc. I saw with an electric start that he was looking directly at people's energy, *seeing* them deeply and immediately. I had never witnessed anyone doing that, although in recognizing his act I also saw my own previously unacknowledged ability. As he looked at people, his seeing invited liveliness. Some people sat up, others shrank away slightly. I saw that Gay's highest interest was life itself. My core lit up with joy, laughter, and bubbling interest. I also thought that Gay was the brightest, funniest man I'd ever encountered. It was as if my inner self woke up and breathed for the first time in Gay's presence. And I could see that he wasn't interested in my surface. He invited my true self into the light before we even exchanged a word. It was a magical moment that formed a base for building a new kind of relationship."

About six months after we moved in together. At the time, neither of us had much money. Gay had been given a buzz-cut by the relentless shears of divorce, while Kathlyn never had any money to start with. We rented a small house in Colorado, where Gay had lived for many years. Our energy in the first year of our relationship went into enjoying each other's company while defining our relationship goals. We spent a great deal of time sitting on the floor of our living room, asking each other "What do you most want?" As we talked and talked and talked, it became clear that there were six major commitments we wanted to make to each other. Once we saw what our wants were, we could begin setting up plans for bringing them into reality. It was an incredibly rich time for us in psychological and spiritual ways, although it would take us another five years to see our financial fortunes grow.

Our first want—we called them co-commitments because we reached agreement on what we were committed to—was to have our relationship be an arena for our psychological and spiritual growth. We wanted to define our relationship as a major—perhaps *the* major—learning opportunity of our lives. We agreed that we wanted to be close to each other and that we were willing to do whatever it took to be close. This commitment meant that we would put the relationship above our respective psychological quirks. We acknowledged that we both had lots of patterns of resistance to love, going way back to childhood, and that we would expect and even welcome these as they surfaced in our relationship. But we committed ourselves to choosing the relationship above any of our resistances to it.

This commitment was incredibly important in the year to come. For during that year we saw all of our patterns come to the surface. For Gay, it had to do with the fear of abandonment and the deep conviction that he was unlovable. For Kathlyn, it often boiled down to her Chameleon persona and the need to sacrifice her own needs to please those around her. There were other patterns, most of which have faded into the mists of the past, but we dealt with them all the same way. We told the truth about them.

Our second commitment was to tell the truth to each other, no matter what. This commitment proved to be awesomely difficult to make good on, but somehow we always did. Throughout our lives, both of us had become skillful at hiding our feelings. It was a deeply ingrained habit to break, but in hundreds of experiences in our first few years of being together, we learned the value of telling the truth. The value, quite simply, is this: Truth produces aliveness. Concealment produces deadness in a relationship. Later we would come to feel that a relationship only exists where two people are telling the truth. Anything else is an entanglement.

A third commitment that became important to us was that we were both committed to our own separate development as individuals. We wanted the relationship to be a facilitator of our autonomy. In the past, we had felt constricted in our relationships, that we had been forced to stifle our individual growth to stay in the relationship. We did not want that to happen in this new relationship. A fourth related commitment was that we both agreed to do whatever we could to facilitate each other's empowerment.

In our first year together we had many opportunities to notice how we did not take complete responsibility for our lives. In many subtle ways, we would try to blame the other person for how we felt or how things were going. For example, we were broke a lot during our first year together. Kathlyn would blame Gay for this state of affairs, and Gay would blame Kathlyn. Both of us had lots of good reasons to support our positions. In Gay's opinion, Kathlyn spent too much on food, for example, while Kathlyn thought Gay was too extravagant in matters of entertainment. One day we woke up. We realized we were using money as a power struggle. We sat down on the floor of the living room and talked it out. We both saw that there was only one way out of any power struggle. Both people have to take complete responsibility for what is going on. As long as there is the slightest effort to find out whose fault it is, no progress can be made. Both people must look carefully into how they are the source of the problem, rather than using the energy to put the finger of blame on the other person. A bolt of lightning hit us: What if we both took full responsibility for having the perfect amount of money? What if we used the energy we were wasting through blaming the other person to look for how we could be more prosperous? That day we began a new, fifth, commitment, one which has served us well ever since. Whenever we find ourselves complaining about something, we look into ourselves for the source, rather than looking for the source of the problem outside ourselves. Whenever something is going on that is not to our satisfaction, we both ask ourselves how we are contributing to the problem. This habit saves a major amount of energy that we then can use in figuring out what we want and how to get it.

As you may recall from last chapter, this assigning of blame is called projection. As humans, we have a great deal of difficulty in acknowledging ourselves as the source of the reality around us. Just as the audience gets caught up in the flickering pictures on the screen, forgetting that the source of the image is not up there, we get lost in our dramas and forget that we are the source of them. We keep our problems alive by the attention we give to them, when that same attention could be used, with a slight shift of focus, in designing something new and better. In our own relationship, it took a great deal of discipline and practice to retrain ourselves to look inside for the source of the problem. It was so tempting to see the problem in the other person! We found, much to our humbling surprise, that it was always when we were most convinced that it was the other person's problem that it turned out to be most clearly our own.

Our sixth commitment to each other was to have fun! We decided that, above all, we wanted to have a good time. No one knows precisely the meaning of life, but surely it is not to have a bad time. Lots of people manage to sit in the midst of heavenly possibility and make a hell for themselves. We decided that, regardless of our external circumstances, we wanted to have a good time in our relationship. When we were not having a good time, we agreed to ask ourselves: Would we be willing to go back to having fun? This decision has served us well through thick and thin. When we made this commitment we lived in a rented house, drove a VW bus, and had about five hundred dollars between us. We started having a great time. Later, when we would get caught up in some problem or another and forget our commitment to having a good time, we would catch ourselves and say, "Well, are we willing to have a good time anyway?" We found that we were in charge of our moods, even though we could not always be in charge of our external circumstances. We learned to have a good time with whatever was going on, and as a result the external circumstances of our lives smoothed out. We learned that we could rechannel the energy that we had previously put into our problems. We put the energy into engaging in creative projects. Now we have several luxurious homes and plenty of financial security, and we are still having a great time.

Actually, one of the most profound learnings of that time was that it is possible to *choose* to have a good time. We realized that in many of our past relationships we had chosen to be right rather than to be happy. Seeing that happiness was a choice instead of something that came from outside was extremely liberating. Of course, we had to choose and rechoose to be happy hundreds of times. Dissatisfaction was a deeply programmed habit for both of us. We both come from families where being happy is probably one of the lowest priorities. In fact, when we began to think about it, we both realized that we had never seen any of our family members happy when we were growing up, except on occasions when they had chemical assistance. So, for us, being happy all the time was a commitment more radical than telling our families that we had become communists, nudists, or worse, Democrats.

Making a commitment to happiness opened us up to one of the greatest life-changing insights of our lives. As we began to focus on happiness, we saw that we could only tolerate it for brief moments. We would be happy, then we would do something to bring us back down. We would criticize or worry or argue so that we could return to a more familiar state of unhappiness. We came to call this habit the upper-limits problem. We had a thermostat setting for how much positive energy we could handle, and the thermostat was set embarrassingly low. As we began to catch on to this problem we began studying carefully the moments of feeling good and how we messed them up. As we did this we began to catch ourselves just as we would mess up. Pretty soon we found alternatives to the upper-limits problem, things we could do to stretch out the times of happiness and positive energy.

Gay recalls a specific moment: "I was standing in the bedroom, looking out the window. I felt great. Kathlyn and I were in superb rapport, I was working on an exciting new writing project, and I was looking out the window at the splendor of Pikes Peak. Suddenly I started worrying about my daughter, in boarding school on the other side of the country. I pictured her being homesick. Crying in a dorm. Perhaps she was even cold. Would she remember to wear a warm enough coat to guard against the brutal New Hampshire winter. What about skiing? Would this be the year she broke her leg? I came to with a start. Wait a minute!—last time I talked to her she seemed happy and fulfilled. Why would I be running this chain of catastrophic thoughts through my mind? I realized that it was the upper-limits problem in action. I was using worry about a child to bring myself down. And it's such a socially acceptable thing to do! You can always get up a good conversation with another parent on the myriad ways children can and have messed up. That day made a difference in my life, being the first time I had spotted so clearly one of my interior mechanisms for making myself miserable. I asked myself: What could I do instead of indulging in the thought? The answer that came through was so simple it made me laugh. Go back to feeling good! So I did. I simply let myself drop back into the feeling of happiness that had been there before I got caught up in my thoughts. It was still there—waiting for me to tune in to it again."

Now, after taking nearly fifteen hundred couples through our therapy program, we make a practice of having them spot their upper limits. We find that there are three major ways that people bring themselves down when they are feeling good. They don't feel their feelings, they don't tell the truth, and they don't keep their agreements. Let's look at these from the negative side first, then turn them around into their positive alternatives. When we're feeling good it is highly likely that some negative feeling is going to come up. Why? Because feeling good has often been followed by some pain in our programmed past. At a recent workshop we had people generate a list of bad things that had happened in their lives when they were feeling good. Here are a few:

- "I was masturbating ecstatically when my mother walked in."

- "I was reading and lost in a daydream when I let some food burn."
- "I was riding my bike without hands for the first time when I crashed."
- "My girlfriend and I would always get into a fight right after making love."
- "I scored a perfect grade on a biology test, then tripped in front of the class on the way out."

On it goes. No wonder so many of us are allergic to happiness, even though we say we crave it more than anything. So one of the first things we learned was to let ourselves feel whatever feelings came up when we were feeling good. We learned to feel them, not act on them. We would be feeling great, then both of us would be scared and start to pull back from closeness. Instead, we learned to let ourselves feel scared. Doing this would return us to the good feeling again. And after a while, the negative feelings quit coming up, as we accustomed our nervous systems to handling more positive energy.

We learned that the fastest way to break through the upper limits problem was to tell the scrupulous, moment-by-moment truth. If we were scared, we would say "I'm scared" or "My stomach is tight." If we were angry we would say "I'm angry." The more specific we were, the better it worked. What never worked was to say our feelings in a way that blamed the other person. In other words, saying something like "I'm mad because you came home late" never seemed to help. We learned to qualify statements to something like "I'm angry, and part of me thinks it's because you came home late." Why? Because we learned that we were never upset for the reasons we thought we were. We would start out thinking we were mad about the other being late, only upon deeper inquiry to realize that it was connected to some old childhood wound. Now and then we would be unable to find any deeper connections, but we learned never to stop looking.

As we got closer, we learned to value letting each other have room to feel all our feelings. We learned to value telling and hearing the truth over protecting our feelings. For example, we were driving back to the place we were staying after a party in California.

In Gay's words, "I had talked to twenty or thirty people during the course of the evening, but one conversation stood out. It was with a beautiful woman in her late twenties who had a softness and intelligence that I responded to. Even better, she had read all my books and was an enthusiastic student of the ideas in them. We talked animatedly for twenty minutes or so, then moved on. As Kathlyn and I were driving home, she asked me some question about the woman and I began to stiffen inside just as I might have in my previous relationship. This time I caught myself, however, and decided to tell the truth as best I could. I told Kathlyn that I had felt really attracted to the woman. Kathlyn felt hurt and scared. She told me the truth about the feelings, identifying some of them as present-day feelings and others as old feelings from childhood. I said that I had no intention of acting on my feelings, but I wanted to make sure she knew about anything I was feeling. We probably talked about an hour, detailing as many of our reactions as we could. At the end of this conversation I felt I had broken through an age-old pattern. My old tendency would have been to get resentful and stonewall it, relying on hostility and denial to get through the situation. Instead I told the microscopic truth, and so did Kathlyn. The result was that we felt closer than ever. We had learned that we could have the space to feel whatever we felt with the other person. We did not have to conceal our feelings or numb them out. We could be all of who we were with the other person.

Keeping agreements became an important learning for us. We discovered numerous examples, many quite trivial on the surface, where we used breaking an agreement as a way of taking the edge off our happiness. For example, we would be feeling great and close to each other, then one of us would "forget" to do something we had agreed to do. Gay would agree to take the trash out, then fail to do it so that we would miss the pick-up day. On another occasion, we were feeling very close and had been for several days. Kathlyn went out to buy groceries and got stopped by a policeman for having an out-of-date inspection sticker. She had agreed to take care of this detail a couple of weeks before. Needless to say, it brought her down from her state of positive energy, not the least because he impounded the car on the spot.

We began to see that the process of these upper-limits problems was much more important than the content. We began to regard them all as ways we limited our positive energy. It became clear to us that the Upper Limits Problem was the only one we really needed to pay attention to. In other words, we were either having a good time, or we were doing some kind of upper-limits number on ourselves. We caught ourselves hundreds of times in subtle ways of bringing ourselves down. We would be happy and close, then we would eat a bunch of ice cream and feel miserable. We would make passionate love, then get miffed at each other for some trivial offense. We must have studied the upper-limits problem for at least two years before we mastered the art of staying in positive energy all the time. Now, after over a decade's practice, we very seldom bring ourselves down anymore. We notice the early warning signs of an approaching upper-limits problem and talk about it before it becomes full-blown.

We have found that taking good care of mind, body, and spirit helps smooth out the up-and-down cycles of positive energy. Our day looks something like this: We get up between six and seven, then spend about fifteen minutes stretching and doing a set of floor exercises we have developed. We meditate for about half an hour, using the TM practice we have been doing for nearly twenty years. We have breakfast—usually fruit for Gay and cereal for Kathlyn—then we both go to our respective studios for an hour or two of writing. We have identical Macintosh LC's so that our computers can communciate easily. Kathlyn begins seeing therapy clients later in the morning, continuing through the day until about seven o'clock in the evening. Gay only sees clients two afternoons a week, spending several days at the university where he teaches graduate students in a therapy program. In the evening we meditate for another half hour before dinner. Three days a week we work out for an hour at our local health club, doing the cardiovascular bikes and rowing machines, a weight machine called the Gravitron and a round of Nautilus. We also have a small gym in our house, so we can get an hour of exercise on bad-weather days when we don't want to go out.

If anyone had told us twenty years ago what it would take to stay in shape in middle age, we would never have believed it. We find that we have to make happiness and health our top priorities. We used to think of things like meditating and exercise as luxuries, things we did if we had time. Now we put those things first because we find that we get a lot more done if we harmonize our minds and bodies on a daily basis. Both of us are recovering sweets-junkies, so we really have to watch our diets carefully. Neither of us has ever been a drinker, so alcohol consumption has not needed modification, but we have found that we have changed our diets completely. Nowadays we eat primarily fruit, vegetables, and whole grains. Twenty years ago a day's feeding always included meat and sweets, usually ice cream. Now, we think of these kinds of foods as occasional items, sometimes only once or twice a year. As a result we feel better than we ever imagined possible. To feel infinitely better in our mid-forties than we did in our mid-twenties is a remarkable achievement to us.

So many couples who come to us for counseling have not chosen to make happiness and creativity top priorities. Their priorities are things like:

- Being right
- Making the partner wrong
- Judging, criticizing, and faultfinding

It is simply a matter of priorities. You get whatever you put first. One of our biggest learnings is that the universe always says yes. If you value being right over being happy, the universe is happy to oblige you. We have not found that people are generally maliciously attached to their incorrect priorities; it is simply that they have not learned a better way. Often we see people seem to wake up when they see the possibility of setting happiness and creativity as their top priorities in their close relationships. Things like being right and faultfinding have a seductive quality to them; people frequently use them like a drug. It is very heartening to watch couples reorganize their priorities toward choosing happiness and creativity. One of the greatest pleasures life has to offer therapists is being with people as they change right before our eyes.

In our own relationship, we have definitely learned that we

get what we ask for. One of the central tasks of our lives is to ask ourselves "What do we want?" on an ongoing basis. Usually we set aside a formal time for doing this at the beginning of each year. During this time we devote an hour a day to working on our goals for our relationship. We post the goals in a public place, so that we and our staff can see them on a daily basis. We want our family and staff to know what we want as a couple so that we can get their support. We monitor our goals constantly, making additions and subtractions as we clarify what we are about.

No one exists in a vacuum. People in close relationships need to cultivate support systems for achieving the goals they want. We have cultivated a network of people who are working toward goals similar to ours. We socialize with those people, talk to them often, and do our best to support each other in reaching for what we most want. We and they have all done the activities that you will have the opportunity to do in the second half of this book. We urge you to carry out the activities thoroughly and thoughtfully. Only by putting these ideas to work for you can you really expect to make a difference in your relationships and the world. In our own relationship, we choose to do these kinds of activities because we have seen the power of choice. We hope you will discover and keep rediscovering that you have everything you need to transform your close relationships. Choose to do the work, and we predict you will be amazed by the results.

Part Two

The Workbook: Your Manual for Transforming Your Close Relationship

....

Introduction

The following activities present an opportunity to effect a meaningful transformation of how you do relationships. The skills you will learn are simple but very powerful. We invite you to work diligently on these processes for as long as it takes you to complete them. One couple worked for six months on just one of the activities before they completed it to their satisfaction! Others have worked on one for ten minutes and felt they'd mastered it. The important thing is to complete each activity assignment, however long it takes.

There was a survey done some years ago with the graduating

class of Yale University. Obviously these were all bright people, and many of them came from prosperous backgrounds. In the survey it was found that 3 percent had taken the time to do something quite simple, while 97 percent had not. Several decades later the survey was repeated with the surviving members of the class. It was found that this same 3 percent of the group was now worth more money than the other 97 percent put together! What was this simple thing that the 3 percent did? They had taken the time to write down their goals for their lives. Many of them had worked out their goals in less than an hour's time, but all had done it. We were impressed when we saw this study, because it supported what we had found as therapists. Couples who actually did their homework—the assignments we gave them between sessions—made rapid progress. Those who didn't stayed stuck.

Consider yourself exhorted, therefore, to sharpen your intentions and your pencil and go to work.* We have benefited from these activities, and we have seen thousands of others grow from doing them. And remember, it is possible to learn and have a good time simultaneously. In other words, enjoy!

Three Places to Look for What is Troubling Your Relationship

You may have picked up this book because you want to enhance your thriving relationship. If so, welcome. We are vitally interested in the outer limits of cocreativity in relationship and have some activities especially for you in the last chapter. Most couples who come to us do so because they feel stuck and are looking for some guidelines to get unstuck. In our work over the past twenty-some years, we have noticed that skills in a trio of areas—truth, feelings, agreements—determine whether the relationship has a foundation for growth. When a relationship is in trouble, we look to these three areas first and ask:

*For some of the activities you'll each need a notebook or journal to record explorations. We'd also encourage you to set aside a quiet, uninterrupted time to learn in.

1. What truth is not being spoken here?
2. What feelings are not being experienced here?
3. What agreements have been broken here?

These seemingly simple questions reveal the core problems in the relationship. When these problems are resolved, entanglements can evolve into enlightening relationships. Note that the following activities also are divided into these three categories of truth, feelings, and agreements.

CHAPTER FOUR

The Activities

ASSESSING YOUR INTIMACY LEVEL

In our workshops and seminars we have discovered that people appreciate a method for determining the current condition of their relationships. We have developed three checklists that help people determine the present truth of the matter. One will help you assess the degree to which your relationship is entangled. The second focuses on the nonverbal signs of entanglement. The third assesses the current potential for enlightening relationship. Take a few minutes to check the statements that are true for you.

The Entanglements Checklist

______ In spite of my best efforts, people around me do not change their bad habits.

______ I do not let myself feel the full range of my feelings. I am out of touch with at least one core emotion, such as anger, fear, or sadness.

______ Anger is a particular problem for me, both to recognize and to express to others.

______ I have difficulty allowing others to feel their feelings. If someone feels bad, I tend to rush in to make it better.

______ I often think my partner's upsets and strong feelings are my fault.

______ I worry about other people's feelings frequently.

______ I have secrets, things I have done and not done that I am hiding from another person.

______ I criticize or get criticized frequently.

______ My strong internal critic nags me and keeps me feeling bad even in times when I could be feeling good, successful, and loving.

______ I try to control other people to make them behave and feel certain ways.

______ I spend a lot of time and energy being controlled or avoiding being controlled by others.

______ My arguments tend to recycle, and one or the other of us often apologizes and promises to do better.

______ It is very important to find out who's at fault in an argument and who is right or wrong.

______ In arguments, I find myself pleading victim or agreeing that it was my fault.

______ I often agree to do things I don't really want to do, feel bad about it, but keep silent.

______ People often don't keep their agreements with me.

______ I feel worried and uncomfortable when my partner moves away.

______ Arguments often feel like life-or-death issues.

______ I find myself withholding things from or lying to my partner.

______ I desperately want my partner's approval.

The Nonverbal Signs of Entanglement

______ My partner's sense of time is a real problem for me. When we're getting ready to go somewhere s/he is always
(a) too fast.
(b) too slow.

______ I get smaller when my partner is around.

______ We seem to frequently get in each other's way.

______ I fidget when my partner is talking.

______ After an evening together with my partner, my body feels tense.

______ One or the other of us seems to be sick all the time.

______ I find myself yawning frequently or short of breath around my partner.

______ My eyes wander when I'm talking with my partner.

______ I'm afraid I'm too much, that I'll bowl my partner over.

______ It's really important to me to have my space, and I worry that my partner is getting too close.

______ I freeze up during sex.

______ I notice I try to make myself bigger when we have a disagreement.

______ I don't like my partner's rhythm in making decisions, but I often don't say anything.

The Enlightening Relationships Checklist

______ I know that I am 100 percent responsible for myself and for creating what is occurring in my relationship.

______ I support my partner in being 100 percent responsible for him/herself.

______ My relationship is an ongoing catalyst for my growth and creativity.

______ I can tell my partner anything.

______ My partner and I support each other through our deepest feelings. It's fine for my partner to feel the whole range of feelings.

______ I feel transparent with my partner and willing to be fully seen.

______ We have inspiring, ongoing fun most of the time.

______ I feel connected with my partner whether we are together or not.

______ I enjoy both times apart from my partner and times of close intimacy.

______ My communication closely matches my experience.

______ It is possible for both my partner and me to have what we want.

______ I look for unconscious patterns as they emerge and am willing to resolve them.

______ I hold myself and my partner in the highest regard.

______ I notice I don't change my behavior around my partner to please him or her.

______ When we encounter problems, my intention is to take 100 percent responsibility, tell the unarguable truth, and to clear up the problem.

______ I experience more and more creativity and productivity in my life.

______ My partner is my equal.

______ I can easily discern what I'm feeling and what I want, even if it's different from what other people feel or want.

______ People keep their agreements with me, and my interactions with others flow smoothly.

______ I am the source of my own value and approval.

THE FUNDAMENTAL COMMUNICATION ACTIVITIES

The central communication skill in close relationship is telling the truth. There are many benefits from being able to tell the bottom-line truth to your partner. First, it increases liveliness in each partner *and* in the relationship. Clear, truthful communication opens a deeper flow of intimacy and love. Second, clear communication that sticks to basic sensations and individual experience stops projection.

Almost all couples who come to us for counseling complain about their lack of communciation. We commonly hear, "Either s/he doesn't understand me, or we don't talk at all." We find that individuals have developed their own private language, a shorthand communication style that *they* understand perfectly and are bewildered if their partner doesn't. For example, Fred may complain, "You know, I just get a little weird at the end of work projects. Carol should just roll with that." Carol may wonder if Fred grows extra body hair and prowls at night when he gets "weird," especially if she's supposed to "roll with that."

We have identified some basic truth skills that greatly enhance the quality of couples' communication. When we talk about telling the truth, we are referring to the ability to communicate the details of what is going on in any given moment in a way that doesn't blame anyone else. In our book *Conscious Loving* we call this skill the microscopic truth because it is a way of seeing and expressing experience that is descriptive and specific rather than interpretive and vague.

Another essential truth-telling skill is taking responsibility to communicate until the other person comprehends your words and your intention. Many people have settled into verbal generalizations such as okay, fine, pressured, nice, better, uptight, etc. These words may be somewhat clear to the speaker but a foreign language to the listener. The assumption that your partner should "just know" what you mean can create unnecessary distance.

Some people are communication victims. They wait for their partners to bring up an issue or topic, then reluctantly respond in a put-upon or passive style. A creative and responsible approach to communication is based on finding the truth, not waiting until it's dragged out of you. For example, when Dan and Judy came for therapy in the midst of a crisis, her main complaint was, "I always bring up things to talk about. Dan was worried about his job for three months before I knew anything about it!" Dan's response: "Well, you never asked . . ."

A common communication problem we hear is, "I don't know what the truth is. Is the truth what I'm feeling, or what I think my partner is ready to hear? Don't I have a responsibility to be sensitive to my partner's feelings?" Many of the activities in this book are designed to identify the body sensations associated with experiencing and expressing the truth as distinct from the body sensations associated with witholding it. From an internal ground of knowing when you are in touch with the truth and when you are withholding, you'll discover that finding the right time for the truth sorts itself out. If you are willing and ready to tell the truth all the time, many of the obstacles to open communication simply disappear.

The most demanding aspect of clear communication is maintaining it in times of conflict and upset, when you are what one man described as "being wedged between a rock and a hard place." If you practice these communication activities over time when conflict is not present, you'll establish some new energy tracks for the stuck times, when most of us tend to revert to familiar patterns.

Truth Telling

These exercises are designed to ground partners at a level of communication that creates closeness and trust rather than confusion and misunderstanding. The criteria for success are: Does this communication stop arguments? Does it increase my sense of aliveness? If not, keep exploring and communicating more basic truths until arguments cease and you both feel lively.

STEP ONE
Telling the Truth

INSTRUCTIONS:

Turn toward each other, make eye contact, and take turns doing your best to tell the truth. Start simply, with things that absolutely can't be argued about. Each person say something that is true, then Ping-Pong back and forth for two to five minutes.

EXAMPLE:

Bob: I feel my nose itching.
Marie: I hear this phrase over and over in my head: "Hurry up, you're not doing this right."
Bob: My shoulders are tense.
Marie: I feel sad.
Bob: I look at you, then want to look away.

Here's an example of what this exercise is *not* about:

Bob: I feel like you're mad at me today.

Marie: You're the one who looks mad.

Bob: The truth is you look kind of down today; you're slouching again.

Marie: I hate it when you criticize me.

Bob: I'm just sharing what's true for me!

STEP TWO

Telling the Truth About Body Experience

Being aware of what is actually occurring is the basis for learning to tell the truth. Many people come to us with the complaint that they have no idea how to tell what is true and what isn't. Years of responding to family roles and societal expectations separate most people from the awareness necessary to discern the truth. We find that this simple activity forms the bottom-line foundation for couples to build a knowledge of unarguable truth.

INSTRUCTIONS:

In an exchange, like a Ping-Pong game, each of you take a moment to notice your body sensations, then take turns describing your experience as specifically as possible. If decision making is an issue for you both, toss a coin to decide who will be Partner A and who will be Partner B. Partner A, close your eyes for a moment and take two full, relaxed breaths. Notice any body sensations from your lower belly to your upper chest. Now open your eyes and describe your expeience to your partner as specifically as you can. When you have finished, Partner B, take a turn. Ping-Pong back and forth for several minutes.

EXAMPLE:

Jane: I feel a tugging sensation behind my sternum.

Tony: I notice myself slouching, and my chest feels heavy.

Jane: I have butterfly feelings in my stomach.
Tony: I notice a bubbling sensation, like champagne bubbles, up the whole front of my torso.

DISCUSSION:

Partners sometimes turn to us after doing this activity and ask, "What do bubbling sensations have to do with this crisis in our relationship?" After assisting thousands of people to communicate at this level, we have learned that body sensation is the foundation for knowing what is true. We don't stop with that level of awareness, but we find it a solid floor on which to build a more intricate exchange of the truth. When couples come in, the conflict is usually muddied by years of generalizations, judgments, and misunderstanding. As people practice this basic skill, they usually find that they can sort out what is really happening much more quickly and in a more friendly fashion.

STEP THREE

Telling the Truth About Inner Experience

INSTRUCTIONS:

Using the same format as in Step Two, expand your awareness to include inner voices, images, and specific thoughts. Begin with Partner B this time. Close your eyes and let your awareness turn inward. Notice any inner experience as you take two relaxed, full breaths. Now gently open your eyes and share your experience with your partner. Switch roles and repeat five to eight times. Do your best to focus on just your inner experience, describing it to your partner.

Continue turning inward and then describing your experience to your partner. Include your awareness of and responses to your partner's sharing *as you experience it inside.*

EXAMPLE:

Jane: [*after closing eyes and turning attention inward*] I'm aware of a slight burning sensation around my eyes and the image of the sun coming up.

Tony: I feel myself wanting to lean toward you, but I start to hold my breath.

Jane: Tears are starting to form at the corners of my eyes, and my hands feel clenched.

Tony: I just heard a voice inside say, "Watch out. Women just want to get their clutches on you."

Jane: [*crying now*] I see the image of a balloon deflating. I think I'm disappointed. I hear my father's voice saying, "Don't get your hopes up."

DISCUSSION:

The central question for most people in close relationships is, "Can I be me and still be with my partner?" We can learn the crucial skill of honoring our experience ***and*** hearing our partner. This activity is designed to differentiate your experience from your partner's so that you can blend your experiences and awareness and your partner's while maintaining an awareness of yourself. The ability to be present to our experience while in the company of another person, especially a romantic partner, is at the heart of building an enlightening relationship. In our seminars, we hear over and over, "I'm really in touch with myself until s/he comes in and asks me for something; then I completely forget to check in with how I'm feeling." If we can't focus inwardly on ourselves we tend to look outside for anchors or direction. This puts us behind the eight ball, subject to any strong fluctuations of mood and energy around us. If we cannot easily focus attention outward, it is difficult to make genuine contact and create intimacy.

STEP FOUR

Telling the Truth in the Moment

This activity expands the flow of awareness to include the environment as well as your partner. It builds on the skills you've learned in the previous activities to respond to the context and the present moment.

INSTRUCTIONS:

Decide who will be Partner A and who will be Partner B. Partner A, first turn your awareness inward toward yourself. Keep your eyes open during this activity. Describe your sensations, thoughts, and images out loud. Then focus on your partner and the surrounding environment and describe out loud just what you notice. Then switch roles. Each of you alternate describing your inward and outward perceptions three times.

EXAMPLE:

Jane: When I tune inward, I notice the thing I'm calling disappointment is actually sadness, a yearning, reaching-out feeling in my chest and arms. When I focus outward, the room seems really big to me, and you seem far away.

Tony: My stomach is contracting into a little ball. I feel restless in my legs. This is familiar. When I turn my attention to the outside, I notice the colors seem very bright, and you look sad.

Jane: I feel a rush of warmth in my chest hearing that. My arms let go. When I look at you, I'm aware of your height. I realize I depend on you to kind of hold me up in life.

Tony: My leg jiggling is slowing down, and my stomach feels like it has a little more space. When I focus outward, I feel connected to you. It's almost like a big bubble that we're both inside. You know, my father was always heading out the door when my mom needed help with us kids. I would like to learn to be here when you feel sad or need something, instead of automatically withdrawing.

STEP FIVE

Telling the Truth about Feelings

The purpose of this activity is to give you a sense of your current ease or difficulty in experiencing and expressing your feelings with your partner. If you find that you can communicate your feelings in the same tone of voice that you would if you were giving someone the time of day, you are a feelings graduate and probably have no charge on any particular feelings. This is rare. If you don't have such a friendly experience of your emotions, the section on sorting feelings may be especially useful for you.

INSTRUCTIONS:

Part One: Using your journal, take several minutes to complete the following sentences. Jot down what you first notice. *There is no right or wrong answer here, just what is true for you:*

- When I feel sad, the body sensations I notice are ______.
- When I feel angry, the body sensations I notice are _____.
- When I feel scared, the body sensations I notice are _____.
- When I feel sexually aroused, the body sensations I notice are ________________.
- When I feel ashamed, the body sensations I notice are __.
- When I am sad, I want to ________________.
- When I am angry, I want to ________________.

- When I am scared, I want to ______________.

- When I am sexually aroused, I want to ______________.

- When I am ashamed, I want to ______________.

- The feeling I hide most is ______________.

- The feeling that is most confusing for me is ______________.

- I am still sad about ______________.

- I am still angry about ______________.

- I am still afraid of ______________.

- I still have sexual feelings about ______________.

- I am still ashamed of ______________.

Part Two: Stand facing your partner and maintain eye contact. Decide who will be Partner A and who Partner B. Take turns saying each of the following sentences. Partner A will begin. Say the first sentence, then pause for two long, slow breaths and notice your thoughts and body sensations. Then Partner B says the same sentence, pausing to notice for two slow breaths. Continue through the whole list. When you come to a sentence with a blank, say whatever emerges first, without rehearsal. Participants in this activity have noticed a strong temptation to do other things besides just saying the sentence and breathing. Here are some examples of things people have felt compelled to do:

- Interrupt the speaker to give their version
- Tell a story about that feeling
- Give their life history
- Edit their partner
- Criticize their partner's delivery

Please notice if you feel drawn toward these responses, or others, and do your best just to say the sentence, breathe, and notice.

- I'm afraid of abandonment.
- I'm afraid of being alone.
- I'm afraid of being engulfed.
- I'm afraid of dying.
- I'm afraid of losing control.
- I'm afraid of getting old.
- I'm afraid of being poor.
- I'm afraid of ______________.
- I'm angry about injustice.
- I'm angry about how I was treated by ______________.
- I'm angry about ______________.
- I'm sad about the way things were.
- I'm sad about what happened with ______________.
- I'm sad about ______________dying.
- I'm sad about ______________.

DISCUSSION:

Expressing and sharing our feelings is one of the most healing aspects of an intimate relationship. When the flow of feelings is open and clear, a balance of harmony and purpose is easily maintained. When feelings are withheld, the relationship founders. Partners in close relationship need to know that feelings are like blood; they circulate through us all the time. If we are able to recognize our feelings and tell the truth about them, physical, emotional, and relationship health follow.

STEP SIX

Telling the Truth About the Past

INSTRUCTIONS:

Part One: Each of you take your journal and write without stopping for ten minutes. Focus on any issues, feelings, or events from the past that have kept coming up in your awareness. You might write about secrets, disappointments, things that you have left incomplete, or anything in your relationship that keeps recirculating inside. As you are writing, let yourself express both your thoughts and images, as well as the body sensations and emotions that come up in connection with these issues. Use a timer so you won't have to focus on the clock.

Part Two: Each of you take a few minutes to rest and notice your responses to writing. Sometimes people notice that this process releases emotions that have been hidden.

Now, decide who will be the communicator and who the listener. Listener, your job is to open your senses fully to your partner's communication, trying on his/her experience as if it were your own. While s/he is speaking, don't interrupt. Communicator, for three minutes share whatever is true for you about your journal exploration. Do you best to stay with your sensations, thoughts, and feelings as you keep returning to what is true. Your communication may or may not have anything to do with your partner. After three minutes, switch roles. Listener, just focus on receiving your partner's communication without interruption. When each of you has shared, take a few minutes to breathe relaxed, full, connected breaths into your belly before returning to your normal activities.

DISCUSSION:

The research of James Pennebaker has demonstrated powerfully the benefit of sharing past traumas and hurts, especially those that have been hidden. His studies have focused on the dramatic health improvement that telling the truth provides. In our work with couples, we have found that the health of the relationship takes a huge leap when partners share traumas that still linger in their awareness. Interestingly, one of Pennebaker's findings is that, while the people who participate in his studies and write about their traumas often feel more emotionally upset when finished, at the same time, their overall health improves immediately. Don't be surprised if you experience more feelings after this activity. That is part of the unwinding process. Most people quickly experience increased harmony, both inside themselves and in the relationship.

The Aliveness Experiment

This activity is designed to explore and contrast telling the truth and withholding the truth. Its simple structure may allow you to feel this difference in your body, to give you a clear distinction between the physical sensations of revealing and concealing.

INSTRUCTIONS:

Decide who will be the first explorer and who will be the first witness. Stand facing your partner and make eye contact. As you begin, each notice the basic level of your aliveness. Notice how awake or sleepy, tense or relaxed you are. Mentally file that information away for later comparison. Witness, you will keep noticing your experience and noticing your partner as you do your best to be with your partner.

Now, explorer, take a moment or two to turn your awareness inside until you locate a sensation that you are experiencing, for example, pressure at your temples or tight shoulders. Get ready to describe this out loud to the witness, but don't. Let that experience go, or file it away somewhere in yourself, and turn your awareness inside until you locate another sensation. Get ready to describe it out loud, but don't say anything. Repeat the experience of locating a sensation, getting ready to communicate it, then withholding five times.

Next, locate another physical sensation and get ready to describe it, but don't. Instead, hold your breath for a moment. Then shake off that experience. Repeat this process five times. Take a moment to notice the level of your aliveness now as compared to at the beginning of this activity. After you have taken the time to notice, switch roles.

Now, first explorer, turn your attention inward until you notice a sensation, then describe it as specifically as you can to your partner (the witness). Describe its qualities, shape, size, texture, weight, motion, and anything else about the sensation you notice. When you feel your description is complete, turn your attention inward again and locate another sensation. Tell the truth about it to your partner. Repeat this process five times; notice the level of your aliveness. After a moment or two, again switch roles.

VARIATIONS:

- Tune in until you become aware of your current emotion, then hide it. Contrast five times of doing that with locating an emotion and sharing it.
- Start to reach out to your partner, then pull back. After repeating that several times, reach out and complete the motion with a hug or touch. Contrast the sensations.

DISCUSSION:

Learning by contrast is a powerful and direct method of promoting growth. This activity uses the natural oscillation of opposing forces to demonstrate opposite ends of a spectrum. Some people learn best by simply moving forward in the desired direction. Others seem to grow most by pushing against a base or backing up before moving forward. Learning by contrast allows us to see and experience both sides of a process. Some of our clients love this activity; others describe it as torture. If you love it, you may wish to use the principle of learning by contrast in the rest of your life. Let yourself fully experience what is currently true before you move into something new. It's like bending almost to the ground before leaping; some people can get very high that way.

Sorting Feelings

In our relationship seminars and couples therapy work, we have noticed that many people get snagged when communicating feelings. Most of us either never learned, or learned faulty feeling models that we carry into other relationships. One faulty model in communication is confusing thoughts with feelings. When people haven't learned to tell the difference between mental and emotional processes, they may use phrases similar to the following:

- "I think I'm scared of you."
- "I feel that you're not spending enough time with me."
- "My feeling is that you're being a jerk."
- "Logically these tears don't make any sense."

Another feeling problem encountered by many people is telling one emotion from another. In our culture it is much more acceptable for men to feel anger than sadness, and we've noticed that many men have trouble making the distinction between those feelings. Men learn to let anger emerge under stress, but the anger often covers other emotions. For example, a man may bellow at his wife when he's actually sad about the situation. Women, in contrast, have learned to express sadness more readily than anger. We count it a success in therapy when the man contacts his sadness directly and the woman learns to feel and express anger in a straightfoward way. Other emotions get muddied up for many people. Anger can get mixed up with fear or sexual feelings. Fear can be covered with the armor of aggressive anger. It can be very confusing to see your partner crying and to know in your gut that she's angry. Or to bring up a scary subject and have your husband explode. No wonder many couples avoid deep feelings altogether.

Did your education include even an hour exploring the range of human emotions? For a brief time in the 1960s and 1970s, some classes sat in a circle on the floor and shared experiences of feelings and explored how to communicate them clearly and in a friendly way. Most of us, however, got our feeling education at home, from the media, and from friends. This informal education is often vague and complicated by the family rules about what feelings are allowed to be expressed, when, and by whom. For example, in one family only Dad can be angry, and everyone is conditioned to placate him. In another family intense feelings are not allowed at all. The message is, "Go to your room until you can be nice."

If we have not been allowed to explore and express the range of possible feelings that humans experience constantly, we often disconnect from the tangible and distinct sensations that feelings produce in the body. The most common complaint we hear in therapy is, "I don't know *what* I'm feeling." If you bring a feeling-starved background into your relationship, the interactions can look like two people searching for a needle in a pitch-dark room. Beginning feeling communciations between partners often sound like this:

- "I've been kind of uptight today—I don't know why."
- "Geez, I'd like to be more relaxed, but I don't feel anything but tense below my neck. And my neck! A block."
- "Mary breaks into tears a lot when I try to tell her something. I don't know what that means, and I usually just shut up."
- "When you get tight-lipped like that, I think you're angry."
- "I'm not angry. I'm just trying to stay out of your way."

Each of our primary emotions creates body sensations and distinct energy tracks through the body. We use the following chart of feelings and their corresponding body sensations to help partners identify and clarify their emotional experience.

EMOTION	BODY LOCATION	POSSIBLE SENSATIONS
Sadness	throat	lump, narrowing
	chest	pressure, aching
	belly	empty
Anger	back of neck	ropes of tension, lumps
	head	throbbing temples, clenched jaw
	shoulders	drawn in tight, blocky

	arms and hands	held back, curled
Fear	belly area	butterflies, fluttering, clutching, heavy ball
	head and face	dizziness
	chest, throat	shortness of breath
	face	tension around eyes, mouth; mouth dry
Sexual feelings	genitals	streaming, fullness
	lower belly	good achy
	front of body	warmth
Joy	chest area	spacious, expansive
	eyes	glowing, clarity
	front of body	bubbling, giggly inside

Take a few moments here to do a short feelings assessment. Use this chart to explore your most recent experiences of sadness, anger, fear, sexual feelings, and joy in terms of the body areas and possible sensations we suggest. Do you have similar sensations, or are your experiences very different? Jot down your own body sensations. Recall the last time you experienced each emotion, and describe your sensations and their locations.

EMOTION	BODY LOCATION	SENSATIONS
Sadness	______________	__________________
___________	______________	__________________
___________	______________	__________________

Anger ______________ ____________________

______________ ______________ ____________________

______________ ______________ ____________________

______________ ______________ ____________________

Fear ______________ ____________________

______________ ______________ ____________________

______________ ______________ ____________________

______________ ______________ ____________________

Sexual feelings ______________ ____________________

______________ ______________ ____________________

______________ ______________ ____________________

Joy ______________ ____________________

______________ ______________ ____________________

______________ ______________ ____________________

Now, reflecting on your emotional experiences, answer the following questions:

Do you favor certain emotions and rarely experience others? ____

____

____

Which emotions do you find the easiest to express clearly? ____

____

____

Most difficult? ________________________________

____

____

Which emotions are easiest to be with when your partner experiences them? ________________________________

____

____

Most difficult? ________________________________

____

____

Do you experience and express your emotions differently when alone than you do when your partner is present? Describe the differences. ________________________________

____

____

____

Is anything about your emotional experience and expression familiar? Did you learn it from someone? ________________

____

____

Would you be willing to experience and express all your emotions in a friendly way? __________________________

____

____

Another major feeling problem in couples' communication is thinking that we have to *do* something when feelings occur. Partners often interrupt each other's feeling cycles and rush in to rescue and soothe, launch into their own incomplete feeling expressions, or engage in other ineffective strategies when deep emotions surface. *We need to understand that the best thing to do with feelings is* feel *them.* Each feeling is like a rainstorm. If we just participate and breathe through them, feelings pass through, leaving a cleansed, open space behind. In contrast, if we stop a feeling cycle, those experiences and sensations don't disappear. They dam up in the body and create all sorts of dis-ease in the individual and in the relationship.

We think it's useful to separate the primary emotions and secondary feelings, rather like colors in a paint palette. The ability to sort out combinations of primary emotions makes their experience more friendly and their expression clearer. People tell us they feel empowered by knowing these distinctions rather than overwhelmed by the interlock of several muddied primary emotions. For example, one man discovered that his guilt about an affair covered the deeper experience of anger at his wife's lack of emotional responsiveness and fear that she would abandon him. He was totally unaware of those distinctions until he sorted out the feelings mixed up in guilt.

Take a look at the following diagram and notice that we have distinguished between primary emotions and experiences that are

PALETTE OF FEELINGS

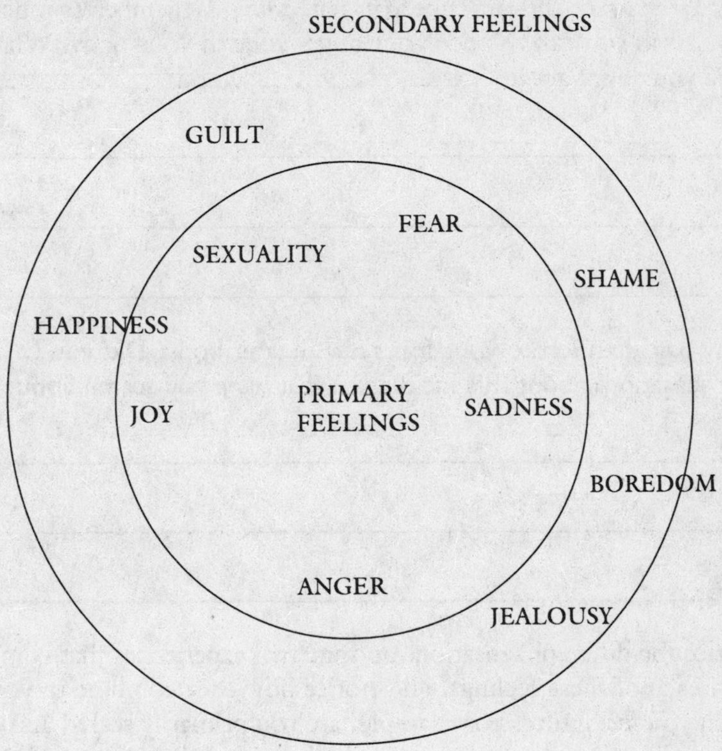

combinations of primary emotions. For example, some people consider guilt an emotion. Guilt is a combination of fear and anger *in different proportions*. The secondary feelings in the diagram are the ones that show up most often in relationships. There may be others that you experience or know. Feel free to add to the palette.

Now that you have explored the sensations of your primary emotions, refer to the diagram above to do an emotional sorting of the secondary feelings.

1. Think of the last time you felt *guilty*. Remember as much about it as you can. Notice your anger zone in your body. What were you angry about? ______________________

____

____

____

Now pay attention to your fear zone in your body. Did you have fear sensations about this incident? What were you scared about?

____

____

____

Notice the different sensations and internal experiences that come with each of these feelings, and notice how they combine in you when you feel guilty. For example, are you primarily scared and a little angry, or primarily angry and a little scared? Let your body experience tell you. ______________________

____

____

____

2. Think of the last time you felt *ashamed*. Let your reexperiencing be vivid. Pay attention to your fear zone and notice your body experience. What are you afraid of? ______________________

____

____

Now turn your attention to the body areas where you experience sadness. Are you feeling sad? Ask yourself what you are sad about and notice how your mind and body respond. ____________

____

____

Notice the different sensations and thoughts that come with the experience of shame and how they combine for you. Is fear or sadness most pronounced? Notice what your body tells you. ____

____

____

____

3. Now remember a recent time when you experienced *jealousy*. Scan your mind and body and notice specific thoughts and sensations that occur with jealousy.

Check the body locations where you experience sadness. Are you sad? Ask yourself what you are sad about and note down your responses and sensations. __________________________

____

____

Notice your anger zone. Are you angry? Ask yourself what you are angry about and notice your thoughts and sensations. _____

____

____

Now check your fear zone for specific sensations that let you know you're scared. Notice how much fear is present and ask yourself what you are afraid of. ______________________

____

____

What proportion is each of these primary emotions in your experience of jealousy? Is fear, anger, or sadness predominant? Do these proportions change if you're jealous in your relationship rather than with another person outside it? ____________

____

____

4. Last, let's look at *boredom,* a secondary feeling that people rarely examine. Boredom can be a rich source of discovery once we've sorted the primary emotions that make up the exquisitely numbing experience we call boredom. Remember as vividly as you can a recent experience of boredom. See, feel, and notice everything you can about it.

Tune in to your anger zone and notice any sensations of anger that are present, however dim. Note down what you sense and any anger thoughts. ______________________

____

____

Scan the places where you experience fear in your body. Are you afraid? Ask what you are afraid of and note down what you notice.

____

____

____

And now notice how anger and fear are mixed in your experience of boredom. Which primary emotion is most noticeable? Do you experience either anger or fear hiding the other? ____________

____

____

____

Make some time now or later to share your discoveries with your partner. Couples who have gained some skill at sorting feelings tell us that exhilaration and lightness take the place of the heavy pull of unexperienced feelings. To be able to know what you are feeling is an important step to communicating clearly in relationship.

The Feeling Inquiry

This exercise was inspired by the memory of interactions with our son Chris when he was three and four years old. I (Kathlyn) had been practicing sharing my feelings with Chris regularly to help him distinguish events that involved him and events that had nothing to do with him. For example, I would say, "I'm feeling irritated today, and it has nothing to do with you. I love you and want you to keep having a good time." Or, "I am irritated with you this morning. I don't want you to pull the cat's tail anymore." Over time, Chris began initiating feeling discussions. He would ask, "Mom, are you sad today?" or, "Mr. Gunnar [his preschool teacher] seems really angry all the time. Doesn't he like kids?" These questions, innocently asked, gave me a tremendous opportunity to be more conscious of feelings and the impact of unexpressed feelings in our lives. This activity is designed to distinguish our feelings from our partner's and to spot the feelings that we have trouble owning so we can stop the cycle of projection.

INSTRUCTIONS:

Decide who will be Partner A and who will be Partner B. Partner A will be the creator and Partner B the responder. Partner A will enact the following list of feelings, and Partner B will share his/her response to each item out loud. Partner A, do your best to use your whole body and voice to make each feeling larger than life. Exaggeration can often bring hidden responses out of the shadows. Take a couple of deep, relaxed breaths after each feeling and shake it off before moving on to the next. Partner B, tune in to your truthful response to each feeling and share that out loud before Partner A moves on to the next feeling.

Partner A, take a few minutes to let yourself look and sound

- *Sad* . . . and Partner B, tell the truth about your response.
- *Fearful* . . . Remain looking fearful while Partner B shares.
- *Annoyed* . . . Do you best to hold an annoyed posture until Partner B shares.
- *Really happy* . . . Partner B, you may be surprised at your response to this feeling.
- *Hesitant* . . . Exaggerate this slightly fearful feeling until Partner B responds.
- *Enraged* . . . Hold your most extreme posture while Partner B tunes in and speaks.
- *Ashamed* . . . Remember a shameful incident and hold that feeling until B is through.
- *Sexy* . . . Think of something sexy and do your best to show sexiness.
- *Serene* . . . Recall a harmonious event and exaggerate the feeling.

Example (of Partner B's responses):

- *Sad* . . . "I can feel myself wanting to take care of you. I can't stand people being sad, and I want to reach out, to do almost anything to make it better."
- *Fearful* . . . "I don't have much response to this one. I can see you being afraid, but it seems easy to tolerate. It's okay for you to be afraid."
- *Annoyed* . . . "I'm getting mad, wow! That's interesting. I remember that in my family everyone was almost always mad about something. It almost got to be a competition about who was the most angry."
- *Really happy* . . . "This is hard to say, but your being really happy makes me sad. I don't think real happiness was very acceptable . . . I haven't seen a lot of it."
- *Hesitant* . . . "Oh, am I supposed to do something here? I can feel a need to fill in the blanks, to assume what is going on for you."
- *Enraged* . . . "This is like the game King on the Mountain for me, this is easy to be with. I think I actually don't take it very seriously, like it's fake."
- *Ashamed* . . . "Ummm, this one is very tough even to be with. I feel squirmy and like I want to run out the door."
- *Sexy* . . . "I hear all kinds of admonitions in my head, like 'Don't be cheap,' 'Nice girls wouldn't do that,' 'Why buy the cow when you can get the milk free?' I have a lot of junk in my head about sexual feelings."
- *Serene* . . . "This is very nice. I have some warm, kind of streaming feelings in my chest and arms. I notice I'm breathing easier."

When Partner A has gone through the whole list and Partner B has had a chance to respond fully to each feeling, switch roles. When you have each enacted and responded to the list of feelings, take some time to note your responses in your journal.

DISCUSSION:

What feelings were most difficult to respond to, and which were easiest? Did you recognize the feelings that get muddy between you and your partner, the ones that you project most often? For example, in practicing this, Kathlyn noticed that when Gay looked angry, she assumed she had done something wrong. Most of her attention then went into a fixing mode, things she could do to soothe Gay's anger. After practicing this activity for a while, she was able to ask, "Are you angry? Are you angry at me?" These simple questions interrupted the assuaging pattern and gave Gay a chance to reflect on his actual feeling in the moment.

Agreements and Aliveness

The subject of agreements raises the temperature in the room whenever we discuss it in seminars. Many people are confused, angry, and ineffective around the issue of keeping agreements. In relationships, the breaking of agreements is right up there with leaving socks on the floor as a major source of conflict. We have heard amusing and heartbreaking justifications for breaking agreements. Everything from "I forgot" to "I won't because you broke an agreement twenty years ago, and I'm still mad about it." On closer examination, we've always found that we break agreements because it's inconvenient to keep them or because we can't separate our anger at authority figures from agreements.

There are several central agreement skills that allow a relationship to move from entanglement to enlightening. The most basic is keeping the agreements you make. We are amazed at the rationales that people invent for breaking agreements. Even a great excuse doesn't erase the breaking of an agreement. The opposite side of the coin is not making agreements that you don't want to make. For example, many people have mentioned a pattern of giving in to requests, then later reconsidering and deciding they don't want to do what they've agreed to do. Not having learned the accompanying skill of knowing how to change agreements if they are not working, they "forget," get sick, are late, do an ineffective job, etc.

Ultimately, we need to learn that keeping agreements increases aliveness and personal power. Many people experience agreements as Big Brother watching them. If we are the source of our agreements, life works and relationship works.

INSTRUCTIONS:

This activity can be completed individually or with a partner. If you are going solo, read the instructions into a tape recorder to listen to while you are in a relaxed state. With a partner, take turns reading to each other. Listener, sit back in a comfortable chair, with your eyes open or closed, and follow the directions.

Reader: "Take a slow, relaxed breath into your center, letting it out with a sigh. Take another long, deep breath into your center and let it go with a sound . . . Notice the sense of aliveness in your body. Are you relaxed, alert, tense, bubbling with good feeling? . . . Now let your mind and body travel through recent time until you discover an agreement you made and didn't keep. Take your time to notice the nature of the agreement. Was it with yourself, a close partner, friend, or business associate? . . . How did you make the agreement? By phone, in person, by assumption? . . . Now notice how your mind responds to looking at the issue of making an agreement and not keeping it. What thoughts, justifications, and beliefs arise? Notice them with a sense of observing a communication appearing on the fax machine or a movie screen. Just be aware of these thoughts . . . Let yourself notice your body sensations as you continue to focus on this unkept agreement. What areas of your body speak to you, and how do they speak? With tension, pressure, aches or pains? . . . Now be aware of any emotions that are present as you think about this agreement. Notice that the emotions may be large and prominent or barely present in your awareness . . . Now scan your body and notice your overall sense of aliveness after focusing on this unkept agreement. Compared to when you began this exploration, do you feel more or less alive? Take a moment to love yourself for all your feelings, thoughts, and sensations . . . Then stretch easily and come back to the room."

DISCUSSION:

To take complete responsibility for agreements we need to experience the connection between keeping agreements and increased aliveness. You may have experienced a specific or general decrease in your sense of aliveness when exploring broken agreements. The contrast to the thrill of integrity can be striking. Until that connection is made, agreements continue to be entangled with issues of authority and rebellion. Very few people like to be told what to do. Agreements are often confused with coercion, even if self-inflicted. Mastery in the arena of agreements is a key relationship and life skill that places you at the helm rather than in tow behind the ship.

Your Relationship Dance

Each relationship is a unique dance, a combination of each person's rhythms of getting close and getting separate. We have discovered that couples have a strong urge to impose order, or control, on what is inherently dynamic and asymmetrical. Each partner has different preferences for times and length of contact and separation. Rarely do these rhythms match. For example, one person wants to get close when the other is longing for time alone. Both want space at the same time, without children. One prefers to approach quickly, careening into intimacy, while the other prefers to take one step at a time and check things out. This asymmetry is natural and vital to the energy of relationship. However, we have a tendency to blame and control. If our partner doesn't get close and separate the way we do, we try to change them, ourselves, or the rhythms. These tendencies can lead to enormous power struggles, but, even more important, tend to flatten the effervescence that an appreciation of difference can bring to close relationship. It's akin to learning the tango, then deciding it would be better with shorter steps and a little more space between bodies. You'd get more order, but the flare and daring of the dance would disappear.

This activity is designed to help you explore your relationship dance consciously. Do you tango or two-step? Do you do a yo-yo boogie that's usually opposite to your partner's? You each probably have a unique dance. That can be one of the joys of close relationship. You may want to name your particular dance after you experience this activity. You will need a room that has enough open space so you won't need to consider obstacles as you are moving.

INSTRUCTIONS:

Both of you will be moving at the same time, coming closer to each other or moving farther away in space. Stay in motion, as fast or slow as you want from moment to moment. As you come closer and move into separate space, notice the following:

- Are you doing what *you* want to do, or are you reacting to your partner?
- Is your preference getting close or getting separate?
- When you move at exactly the right speed for you, what do you notice?
- Do you notice any patterns in your dance?
- Would you be willing to celebrate your unique relationship dance?

DISCUSSION:

Partners who have experienced this activity are amazed at how much meaning they have attached to their version of getting close and getting separate. Here are some of the responses people have expressed:

- "When George starts to move away, I have this knee-jerk response: 'See, he doesn't really love me!' "
- "I find myself trying to match Cindy, to notice her clues and follow them. God, that's disgusting!"
- "I suddenly remembered episodes of 'cutting the pie' at our house. The three of us kids would have endless arguments over who got to cut the pie, were the slices exactly even, and who got to choose first. I'm obsessed with things being

fair, and I guess I've carried that over into my marriage, even to when we each take space."

- "Once I let go of being right, I began to notice this lovely rhythm to our being together. I appreciated both the coming together and the moving apart. Each phase has its own integrity and a kind of grace."

This activity may bring to awareness the phases in your relationship dance that need your loving attention.

The Bottom Line

When couples come into therapy to sort out the difficulties that have clouded their bond, we often find that they have lost sight of what is essential in the relationship. Each day brings its particular load of what we call the "necessary but trivial" items of life: the errands, phone calls, cleaning, and maintenance that uphold the structure of the home or workplace. There are problems with getting lost in the necessary but trivial and losing sight of the bigger picture. Daily pressures or the little irritations of life can distract couples from a felt connection to the reasons they got together in the first place. And they forget one of the central reasons we join with a particular person: We come into relationship to complete some part of ourselves we haven't claimed. When our partner's behavior reflects that unowned part back to us, we usually become indignant or judgmental. We forget that part of the initial relationship contract called for her/him to behave in just the ways that will illuminate our shadow areas.

This is a sorting-out process. We find that many couples have not openly considered what the bottom line is in their relationship, the things that are essential to make a foundation for growth. These things are distinct from the "would be nice" category of traits and behaviors. Essential characteristics are the water and nutrients of a relationship, without which it will wither.

INSTRUCTIONS:

In your journal each of you independently makes a list of what is essential to you in a relationship. What are the things that bring you satisfaction and joy and make it possible to support your partner in her/his purpose?
For example: A partner who

- is willing to look at issues and let go of positions easily
- has a sense of humor
- is curious about life and the way the world works
- asks for what s/he wants instead of expecting mind reading
- has a deep commitment to growth and spiritual fulfillment

Or on the more practical level: A partner who

- is responsible, who will pick up after him/herself, for example
- shares tasks
- keeps agreements without hassles

When you have completed your lists, share them with your partner. See if there are any surprises. Use some sharing time to remember what brought you together originally. Notice if any changes in your expectations may call for a change in your assumptions and agreements with each other. People in relationships often grow at different rates. Knowing the bottom line can help center you in what is essential to your connection and what can give a little.

The Enlightening Relationship Two-step

The mind-reading problem and the ostrich problem bog down many relationships. The mind-reading problem involves not seeing or saying what we want because our partner should already know if s/he really loves us. The ostrich problem is not seeing how it is or saying how it is and pretending that others can't see either. This dysfunctional relationship two-step creates untold misery and can bog us down very quickly. Simply put, we don't get what we want and need because we fail to acknowledge the truth and to express our wants and needs effectively. This process can take the following forms:

HOW IT IS

NOT SEEING HOW IT IS	NOT SAYING HOW IT IS
Won't look at it	Get upset
Pretend it's some other way	Mistake uproar for action
Distort it	Dramatize it
Project it	Project/Blame

WHAT I WANT

NOT SEEING WHAT YOU WANT	NOT SAYING WHAT YOU WANT
Let others tell you what to want	Don't say what you want
Don't think about what you want	Think others can guess what you want
Pretend you don't want anything	Say what you think others want
Think wanting is bad	Say what you don't want

The way to climb out of these bogs is very simple. Acknowledge reality and express your desires effectively. In other words, see your life as it is, then put your energy into creating what you want. The following exercise will help you to verbalize both how things are in your relationship and how you want them to be.

INSTRUCTIONS:

Stand facing each other. You'll have a verbal Ping-Pong game in which you'll take turns completing the following sentences out loud:

- "How it is, is ________________."
- "What I want is ________________."

Complete both sentences before your partner's turn. Begin with what we call the realm of *stuff,* material things—cars, appliances, toys, things for your children.

EXAMPLE:

- "How it is, is I have a dining room table with chipped legs that's too small for entertaining."
- "What I want is an expandable handmade table with drop-leaf sides."

- "How it is, is the car's tires are nearly worn through."
- "What I want is four new radial tires at an incredible bargain."

Exchange four or five rounds of how it is and what I want in the realm of stuff, then move to the realm of your *relationship*. Look at emotions, time together, handling chores, the qualities that are important to you. Exchange four or five rounds of how it is and what I want.
Example:

- "How it is, is I get mad about doing most of the household chores and expect you to know that I want your help without my saying anything."
- "What I want is for you to take charge of the dishes when I cook, to sort your laundry, to share the cleaning, and to empty the trash when it's full."

Now move into the liveliest areas, *sex* and *money*. Be sure to state how it is and what you want. You'll have had some practice by the time you reach these more emotionally laden issues.

EXAMPLE:

- "How it is, is I usually feel too tired at night to make love."
- "What I want is to make love at different times during the day, with an abundance of energy."
- "How it is, is I feel scared we aren't going to have enough money at the end of the month."
- "What I want is enough money to do everything I want and need."

Notice that both the mind-reading and the ostrich problem can be resolved in exactly the same way, by acknowledging reality and expressing your desires effectively. Couples find that communication becomes much easier with a little practice in this essential area. We call this doing the Enlightening Relationship Two-step.

EXPERIMENTS IN GETTING CLOSE

The only commonality among a group of successful writers was this: They made time each day to sit in front of a typewriter or word processor and write. Similarly, the primary condition for becoming a philosopher is setting aside a period of time each day to think. Time can translate into success. By devoting time to the job of writing, the writers achieved success. A relationship is also a job, albeit one for which most of us have deficient or insufficient training. Imagine the success in your relationship that could come with making the choice to focus time and attention on your being together each day. It is within that context that these activities are structured. They are designed to help you to realize that relationships are more than just hard work or another place where you punch the time clock. Each activity is structured to bring light and awareness to new possibilities of contact and creativity in ways that are fun and friendly. We realize that not everyone's first priority is friendly fun, especially in relationships, but having read this far, you may be ready for the challenge of a relationship that really thrives. We invite you to consciously block out fifteen to twenty minutes each day to nurture your relationship, and to guard that time. The benefits will be surprising.

Choosing Closeness

Enlightening relationships are primarily about choice. Each time we consciously choose to open up to new experiences and more intimacy, our inner selves are empowered and freed to support us. Some partners find that, given the choice, they aren't really interested in the same things. This awareness, although painful, creates clarity and the opportunity to make decisions that empower both, rather than struggling in the mud of confusion. When we choose to be close, intimacy is enhanced by the free attention we can bring to the exchange. Playfulness and creativity result, as well as a sense of excitement about the unfolding discovery of each other.

INSTRUCTIONS:

You and your partner stand facing each other, maintaining eye contact. Take turns saying this phrase out loud: *"I am willing to be close to you."*

After each repetition, pause for two to three deep, full breaths. Take four or five turns saying this phrase.

Then say this phrase out loud: *"I choose to be close to you."*

After each repetition, pause for two to three deep, full, breaths and notice your thoughts, sensations, and emotions. Tell the truth about what you notice. Say the phrase, pause to notice, then report your experience. Switch back and forth several times.

Lastly, say this phrase out loud: *"I am willing to clear up any obstacles to getting close in a way that is totally friendly."*

Take turns saying the phrase, pausing to notice, then describing your experience. Avoid stories, analysis, or judgments. Just notice what's there and report it as simply as possible. Switch back and forth five to seven times.

DISCUSSION:

The conscious decision to be close can unearth the fears and hesitations arising from past experience. A couple we worked with recently came in with a recycling problem. They would get close, then have a fight, a common issue we encounter in our work. When we asked them to make a conscious decision about whether they wanted to be close or not, Charlie said, "Boy! I just don't know. My only experience of getting close is thinking I'm going to do it wrong, that Nina will come at me, finger pointing and accusing." We spent some time helping Charlie identify his first experiences of feeling wrong when he got close. He began to see that his experience of conflict might not even be *his* as he remembered the constant conflict between his parents. At that point we came back to the original question in this way, "If it were possible to be close in a new way that didn't involve this old pattern, would you be willing to be close?" At that point, Charlie's face lit up as he opened up to the possibility of choosing intimacy in a new way. Nina visibly relaxed and smiled as she also declared her willingness to get close in a new way.

Exploring Getting Close

We include several journal activities in this book to give you different experiences of focusing on relationship. Some people find verbal communication most helpful; others enjoy the movement processes. Many people find that the quiet activity of journaling allows them to open to deep feelings and experiences in a safe way. Some people have reported that they experience journal activities as filling the inner well so that they are replenished in relationship. See how you respond to this and other written explorations.

INSTRUCTIONS:

Complete the following sentences with whatever occurs to you.

- When I think about getting close to you, I experience ________________.

  (e.g., goose bumps; thoughts about being careful)

- Picturing us being close is ________________.

  (e.g., somewhat fuzzy; arousing)

- When I think of (or picture) you coming closer to me, I experience ________________.

  (e.g., myself shrinking a little; myself smiling and getting taller)

- When I think about staying close to you, I experience ________________.

  (e.g., sadness as I remember the decades of dullness between my parents)

- The main obstacle to being close whenever I want to is ________________.

  (e.g., my worry that you'll hem me in; that there won't be enough time)

- The feelings that come up for me when I get close to you are ________________, and ________________, and ________________.

  (e.g., joy, anxiety, sadness)

- I learned how to get close from ________________.

  (e.g., watching my grandparents' interaction all my childhood)

- I'm afraid that if I get really close, ________________.

(e.g., something bad will happen; you'll see who I really am and not love me)

- Some things I need in order to be close are:

  ____

  ____

  ____

  ____

  (e.g., I need to have a regular time to talk with you about whatever is going on. I need about fifteen minutes to myself when I come home from work to make the transition and let go of the rest of the day.)

- I am willing to make these arrangements about getting close with you:

  ____

  ____

  ____

  (e.g., I am willing to set aside time in my appointment book each day to be with you. I am willing to help with the daily stuff so that neither of us feels as pressured. I am willing to keep discovering how to be closer to you.)

When you have each completed these sentences, take time to share what you discovered. Be aware of responses that were surprising or new, as well as those that seem to have a long history. Together, choose and implement one of your agreements.

Moving Closer

For those of you who like to move together, here is an opportunity to do just that, a different sort of relationship minuet.

INSTRUCTIONS:

Decide who will be the first mover and who the first witness. Witness, keep taking deep, relaxed breaths and notice your experience. Mover, begin standing about ten feet away from the witness. Take one step at a time toward your partner. Stop with each step to report out loud your sensations, emotions, and thoughts; *keep telling the truth about your experience until you feel more lively inside.* Then take another step closer and repeat the process until you are standing right in front of your partner. Remain in eye contact for a few silent moments, then switch roles.

EXAMPLE:

Hank's experience: "You look far away at this distance . . . I notice I'm wondering how you feel about me . . . my chest just tightened a little . . . The thought, "Will I be trapped if I get too close?' just came up . . . I feel warmth in my face and hands . . . I realize I love you and I'm afraid of getting close."

DISCUSSION:

Partners are fascinated to discover how much of their communication about getting close (and separate) is nonverbal. People have unearthed childhood memories and hurts that they hadn't realized were clouding their intention to be close in the present. For example, a number of people have recalled high school dances and the humiliation of crossing the dance floor for a prospective partner, only to be rejected.

Both positive and negative moods are quickly and powerfully communicated between people. Recent research indicates that moods and emotions are transmitted within milliseconds, much too fast to consciously control. Further, several researchers are documenting the effect of an exchange between more and less expressive persons. The more expressive person's mood is almost contagious, picked up instantaneously by the person who is more easily affected. We have often noticed the subtle dance of feeling between people in relationship. This research substantiates our sense that relationship harmony is largely a result of the nonverbal dance. Dr. Frank Bernieri's research has led him to assert, "The degree to which people's movements seem orchestrated determines how much emotional rapport they feel." (*Denver Post,* 10/20/91).

Breathing Together

Are you and your partner able just to be together without doing something or creating a task or a problem to solve? Some couples are able to share a quiet space of silence and feel exquisite sensations between them. Another couple left alone in our office for two minutes immediately recycled an argument that had been raging for decades.

This activity is designed to cultivate a way to grow together at an essential level.

INSTRUCTIONS:

Sit comfortably, facing your partner. Be close enough that you could reach out and touch each other, but for now, remain separate. Throughout this activity, remain in eye contact. Give yourself permission to experience fully the feelings, sensations, and thoughts that may arise for you or your partner.

Each of you rest your hands comfortably on your belly. Each inhalation should gently lift your belly so that your hands also rise. As you breathe out, your hands will fall with the release of air from your belly. Notice if the top of your in breath rolls easily into the out breath. If there is any gap or holding between in breath and out breath, allow the breath to be connected. Continue taking deep, relaxed, connected breaths for two to three minutes.

Let your hands rest at your sides now as you both continue gentle belly breathing. Let yourselves imagine a circle of breath flowing between you. You'll take in breath through your nose and send it back to your partner, as if through your navel. Just imagine this circle of breath flowing easily between you for several minutes as you maintain eye contact.

Now place a hand on your partner's leg or belly, whichever is easy to reach while staying comfortable in your chair. As you continue belly breathing with eye contact, notice your experiences. There is no right experience here. Notice and appreciate whatever occurs. Continue belly breathing with eye contact and touch for two minutes.

Then take a moment or two to lean back, close your eyes and rest quietly. Notice your thoughts and sensations. After a short time, stretch comfortably and open your eyes. For this activity we suggest bypassing any discussion or analysis. Just go on about your day when you feel complete.

DISCUSSION:

When you have practiced the skill of breathing together for a while, you may notice that your focus shifts from the content of your communication to the process. Couples have experienced being able to breathe through feelings and negative thoughts without getting stuck in habitual responses. For example, Ned and Toni noticed that one feeling problem would arise whenever one or the other began to experience emotions such as sadness or fear. The other partner would inevitably say or do something negative, and the feelings would abruptly halt. This pattern had created a history of distancing and assumptions that kept Ned and Toni from being close. After practicing breathing together for several weeks, Toni noticed with some surprise that they were choosing to breathe through feelings rather than choosing the old pattern.

EXPERIMENTS IN AUTONOMY

Getting Separate

Getting separate is as important to an enlightening relationship as knowing how to be close. Most couples we've worked with have learned to equate getting separate with abandonment. The thought, "If s/he really loved me, s/he'd want to be with me all the time," is very common. So is, "If I want time for myself, am I a bad partner? Does it mean something is wrong with our relationship?" Enlightening relationships thrive on each person's direct relationship with the world. Each partner can bring the increased aliveness of creativity, new information, and different contacts to the evolving life of the relationship. However, most of us have a lot to learn about the healthy process of getting separate. These activities are designed to develop a true sense of autonomy between equal partners.

Here's an example of how separateness and abandonment get fused in our minds. In a recent group, participants were exploring ways to feel separate from Mother, since Mother is often the first person from whom we want and need to be autonomous. We were asking what keeps us tied to an old dependent relationship with Mother that doesn't remotely fit the current circumstances of life. When we structured an activity to have one partner respond to the other in positive, negative, and neutral ways, all the participants said that their partner leaving was the most painful experience. Being left was more painful than being yelled at or ignored. We seem to have all kinds of feelings tied up with someone leaving. Here are some of the things participants said when their partners left:

- "I *knew* she was just following the instructions, but I felt she didn't like me."
- "I found myself wildly thinking of ways to entertain her so she wouldn't leave."
- "I noticed that I really shut down. I thought, 'Well, I'll show you I don't need you either!' "
- "I just got numb. I don't know what happened—it's like I went blank."

In close relationships we have noticed that partners' early experiences with getting separate bleed over into their current relationship, and naturally so. A close relationship can be the ground for studying and clearing up anything in the way of a harmonious relationship dance. The following are examples of problematic behaviors that partners use to get separate:

- Turning back on partner
- Shutting eyes while partner is talking
- Walking away (including walking away in middle of partner's sentence)
- Sighing and looking away
- Interrupting when partner is speaking
- Tensing up and holding breath

All these styles are problematic because they are not truthful, direct, or straightforward. Each contains multiple levels of communication that can easily be misinterpreted. As you move through the following activities, be aware of your unique indirect ways of getting separate.

You may also notice as you explore separating that your intention in taking space influences the quality of interaction. Also, your communication about taking space and getting separate can support or stymie the free pendulum swing of intimacy and autonomy.

Journal Activity

Fill in the blanks:

- When I think of myself as an independent person, I feel __________.

  (e.g., exhilarated, but scared)

- The main thing I learned about being autonomous was __________.

  (e.g., people won't like me if I'm too aloof)

- I am afraid of being independent because ________.

  (e.g., nobody will be there when I need them)

- My family told me that independent people were ________.

  (e.g., snobs who thought they were better than everybody else)

- The main thing I need to clear up to become autonomous is ________.

  (e.g., learning to ask for support when I need it; catching the early clues that I need to take space)

Now take a separate sheet and ask yourself, "How am I perpetuating this old pattern in my current relationship?" Take each of the previous questions and bring it into the present. For example, "I currently get exhilarated and scared when I think of myself as an independent person when my partner goes on business trips and I'm responsible for the whole house, the kids, and my work."

When you are both finished, take some time to share your discoveries.

DISCUSSION:

One benefit of this activity is the deeper discovery of your partner's actual experience. I (Kathlyn) remember being amazed to learn that for some time at the beginning of our relationship Gay would feel a twinge of abandonment when I would leave the room to do something. I had this image of Gay as totally self-sufficient (which he is) that didn't allow for any vulnerability. Gay was surprised to find that I felt especially nervous and needy in big crowds, where he was right at home. With the knowledge of how your partner gets separate and has experienced getting separate, you can begin to make more conscious choices in the way you increase your autonomy-closeness balance.

The Autonomy Clues

Here are some examples of signs clients have experienced when they needed to get separate and take some space.

- George felt hemmed in or pressured to the extent that his attention was distracted from communication and closeness with his wife. He found himself daydreaming about fishing alone at dawn on a quiet pond.
- Terry experienced a lot of irritated thoughts, for example, "People are just being too demanding."
- Merrill found himself criticizing his partner more frequently for things that he generally didn't notice. When Pat left his socks on the floor and Merrill saw them on his way to do the dishes, he exploded.
- Cheryl began to wonder if Sam was limiting her freedom and growth. "If only he didn't push me so hard all the time; I never have a free moment to myself."

INSTRUCTIONS:

Take turns saying this phrase out loud several times: *"I am willing to be separate and develop my full potential as an individual."*

Pause for two full breaths each time after you say the phrase and notice your response.

Now take turns repeating this phrase out loud several times: *"I support you in developing your full potential as an individual."*

Pause for two full breaths after each repetition and notice your response.

Take a few minutes to share your responses to these two intentions. Did you experience fear when your partner was speaking? Is the potential for separate growth confused with abandonment or rejection? Did your body respond, for example, with twitching or tightness? Did other thoughts intrude and take your attention away, like what you might have for dinner? Or did you experience increased aliveness and happiness with this activity? There is no right response. Noticing is the important step.

Now see if you would both be willing to make some concrete

agreements about getting separate. Do you need regular time by yourself? Do the clues that you need some space elude you, while rearing up in your partner's face? For example, the authors have noticed that each is usually more skilled at noticing the subtle signs that the other needs space. Kathlyn will notice Gay's forehead furrowing slightly and his sentences getting more clipped when he needs time alone. Gay notices Kathlyn speeding up and getting tidier, but more tight-lipped. We have an agreement to share these observations with each other, which smooths the process of getting separate and taking space.

Here are some examples of agreements that couples have made:

- Mary takes Monday evenings to get a massage, and Dan makes dinner and puts the children to bed. Dan hikes up in his favorite mountain passes on Saturday mornings.
- Betty and Walter have a "time-out" agreement. When either notices the signs of too much closeness, one or both take a half hour with no communication, including on the phone. Sometimes a bath seems just right, or backyard cloud watching.
- Nancy and Donna opt for solo walks when the need for autonomy arises. They notice how refreshing these breaks are and how exciting the relationship looks after a brisk walk.

Learning to Take Space

Most of us haven't had the opportunity to communicate our needs and desires about getting separate in a clear and effective manner. This activity is structured to give you a chance to practice the skill of taking space in a friendly way. We will use the Basic Manifestation Activity as the basis for communication. In the BMA, we acknowledge reality and declare what we want. This combination of skills will allow you to recognize your personal signals for needing space and suggest ways of putting insight into action effectively.

Fill in the blanks in the following sentence (as many examples as you like):

How it is, is___________________, and what I want is_______

Examples:

- How it is, is I feel slightly irritated, and what I want is a long, hot bath.
- How it is, is I have been thinking you're crowding me, and what I want is a half-hour quiet time in the living room by myself.
- How it is, is work is a zoo right now, and what I want is a walk right after I come home from work, before getting into family activities.
- How it is, is both kids were off the walls today, and what I want is for you to make dinner while I take a nap.
- How it is, is I don't know what I want; I'm confused. What I want is about fifteen minutes to just sort things out.
- How it is, is I have been feeling better than ever in my life, and what I want is a quiet evening to rest and integrate that good feeling.

ESTABLISHING THE FOUNDATION: THE INTENTIONS AND AGREEMENTS ESSENTIAL TO AN ENLIGHTENING RELATIONSHIP

In this section we will explore owning and acting from the essential agreements that help relationships flourish. These intentions create a safe and spacious framework for building the relationship you want, while healing any entanglements from the past. With these intentions we focus on creating a spirit of willingness. The experience of willingness is a powerful and friendly catalyst for growth. Willingness, rather than will, opens the maximum potential for the creative juice of the universe to enliven and transform even the driest issues. As you work through these activities, notice the difference between being willing and trying hard. We think you'll be pleasantly surprised that learning can be fun and full of ease.

Journal Activity

Each of you take a blank page in your journal to write out the following intentions. Leave an inch or two of space between each sentence.

- I am willing to be totally independent and totally close.
- I am willing to have my relationships be a force that takes me to my full enlightenment.
- I am willing to clear up anything in the way of my full enlightenment and ability to be close.
- I am willing to have other people be fully empowered in my presence.
- I am willing to transform myself in whatever ways are necessary to serve my highest evolution and have the highest quality relationships with others.
- I am willing to take space as often as necessary to nurture myself and the relationship.
- I am willing to have our relationship be about giving and receiving maximum positive energy.

Now take some time to answer the following questions for each intention:

- *When I say this intention silently, what body sensations do I notice?* Notice if muscles tighten or ache when you repeat these intentions. Does some body part "speak" to you with pressure, tingling, or another sensation? Do you get sleepy, or agitated? Write down whatever body experience you notice.
- *With what beliefs have I surrounded this intention, based on past experiences?* We each come to current relationships with a host of beliefs, most of which are both unspoken and unconscious. Let yourself search for the thoughts that have a quality of cer-

tainty. For example, a common belief is, "If you really loved me, you would always__________." Or, "Once you're married, everything changes (for the worse)."

- *What models, positive or negative, do I have for this intention?* You may have seen relationships in which respect and creative fun were the norm. You may only have seen relationships that seemed to sanctify misery. Or you may not have clear models at all. Notice if one or more intention was modeled in a particular way. For example, the man of one couple saw a relationship model of tight-lipped hostility rather than of giving and receiving positive energy. The woman's model in her family was have an argument, then have sex or buy something. You can imagine the interplay between these styles.
- *What rules have I made about this intention?* For example, many couples have a rule that taking space must happen after an argument or conflict. They do not have rules about taking space in a friendly way. Other couples have unspoken rules about equality in their relationship. Only one person at a time can feel powerful and effective. Write down the rules you have evolved about each intention.
- *Am I interested in living and breathing this intention? What occurs when I imagine this intention being a reality in my life?* We have worked with many people whose attitude is, "Well, theoretically I can see your point. But I think I'll wait for more data." In other words, I'm not willing to step into the arena and actually play the game. These intentions take fire with the risk of action.
- *What action can I take now to continue exploring this intention?* Any action, one step or a giant leap, can have equal power to enliven your relationship. Telling the truth about your experience of relationship modeling is an example of a step. Making a new agreement about taking space is another. What action would you be willing to take as a commitment to your intentions?

Communicating Intentions

In this activity you'll take this exploration of intentions one step further by communicating the intentions to your partner. We'll ask you to communicate in a number of different styles to notice the difference between the direct truth and less effective, but popular forms.

INSTRUCTIONS:

Stand facing your partner. Throughout, take turns saying one intention before moving to the next. Take a couple of breaths between each turn to notice your responses.

- I am willing to be totally independent and totally close.
- I am willing to have my relationships be a force that takes me to my full enlightenment.
- I am willing to clear up anything in the way of my full enlightenment and ability to be close.
- I am willing to have other people be fully empowered in my presence.
- I am willing to transform myself in whatever ways are necessary to serve my highest evolution and have the highest quality relationships with others.
- I am willing to take space as often as necessary to nurture myself and the relationship.
- I am willing to have our relationship be about giving and receiving maximum positive energy.

First round: Each of you mumble and look everywhere except at your partner as you say each intention.

Second round: Say each intention in an angry tone. Experiment with sarcastic, irritated, hostile, outraged, or another variation of angry.

Third round: Communicate with the belief that the situation is hopeless.

Fourth round: Do your best to be direct, straightforward, and clear with each intention.

Fifth round: Say each intention, then take two breaths to notice whatever body experience you had. Exaggerate your response for a moment as you say out loud the truth about what you're noticing. Then it's your partner's turn.

EXAMPLE:

"I am willing to have other people be fully empowered in my presence. My shoulders are rising, and I feel myself wanting to disappear, so I'll bring my shoulders up almost to my ears and go stand absolutely still in the corner . . . As I do that, I remember the arguments my parents had, when I'd hide in my room. My dad always called my mother a mother hen, to which she'd salute and bark, 'Yes, Sergeant!' I don't know what it would look like for both of us to be powerful. But I'd like to have the experience."

Sixth round: Let your focus be on listening closely and receiving your partner's communication, both verbal and nonverbal.

Envisioning the Future

Our purpose in this activity is to make a space for a new future to unfold. We have found that relationships are most effective when each person starts from the present. The agreements and intentions you create will pull you into a new future of unlimited possibilities.

INSTRUCTIONS:

Decide who will relax and receive first, and who will read the following. Receiver, sit back in a comfortable chair and close your eyes if you feel ready to do so. Some people enjoy having soft music in the background for this activity. Reader, take a moment to be with yourself and appreciate yourself for whatever you are experiencing right now. When you are ready, read the following out loud to your partner.

"Relax your belly as you exhale. Allow the in breath to just happen naturally . . . and continue relaxing your belly through the out breath . . . Let your attention move gently through your body. Notice whatever you are experiencing right now . . . Be with yourself as you experience your sensations and emotions. Say yes inside to whatever you experience . . . Now imagine yourself walking through a meadow . . . Notice the colors and the feel of the sun and breeze . . . Take several moments to explore the meadow . . . As you come over a rise you see a pond . . . Go sit by its edge and look into the water . . . As you notice the ripples and reflections, see yourself being and acting confidently with these new intentions.

"*I am willing to be totally independent and totally close* . . . Imagine how our relationship will look as you easily get close and separate.

"*I am willing to have my relationships be a force that takes me to my full enlightenment* . . . Let yourself experience our relationship as an essential part of your full growth and potential. Let your creative self envision how it will be.

"*I am willing to clear up anything in the way of my full enlightenment and ability to be close* . . . Now and in the future any obstacles can be resolved easily and in a friendly way for you and everyone around you.

"*I am willing to have other people be fully empowered in my presence* . . . Let yourself imagine us as truly equal. See you and me being totally responsible and fully empowered.

"*I am willing to transform myself in whatever ways are necessary to serve my highest evolution and have the highest quality relationships with others* . . . Imagine being committed to change and the natural flow of life . . . Notice the thoughts and images that support you to receive feedback from all of life to continue growing and loving.

"*I am willing to take space as often as necessary to nurture myself and the relationship* . . . Create an experience of taking space in a way that celebrates your wants and the relationship . . . Take a couple of relaxed breaths and imagine yourself doing something that is just right for you and me.

"*I am willing to have our relationship be about giving and receiving maximum positive energy* . . . See or feel an image of fun, creativity, and celebration . . . Know that you are the source of this experience and can give and receive love and joy freely and fully.

"Now come back to the side of the pond in the meadow . . . Take a few minutes to appreciate its beauty and explore any last places you want to visit . . . Gently say good-bye to this place for now and let your awareness return to your body and the experience of sitting in the chair. Take a few moments to stretch easily and come back to the room. Open your eyes when you are ready."

Receiver, take a few minutes to record your experiences in your journal. Then switch roles.

DISCUSSION:

One of the most important tasks in an enlightening relationship is making space for something new to occur. Entanglements can get us so twisted into the quicksand that we sink deeper the more we struggle. Taking time to envision a new possible future establishes a brand-new dynamic of ease and relaxation that contrasts with the experience of "working on" the relationship.

THE PERSONA WORK

The following activities will flush out your major personas. These are ways of being and acting that we develop, usually early in life, to cope with difficult situations. Personas can be useful when they are connected to our essential selves. In these activities you'll learn to clarify the persona(s) that are predominant in your life and relationships. You'll also have the opportunity to inquire into who you are under all the layers of your programming. It is important to acknowledge and befriend our personas so we have them, rather than them having us. And ultimately, we want to love all aspects of our personas so that we can build the relationships we want based on choice, not on the unconscious demands of an unresolved persona.

We invite you to have fun with these activities. Our seminar participants find this work exciting and surprisingly helpful.

The Persona Worksheet

STEP ONE

Take a look at the following list of sample personas. See if you recognize familiar attitudes and experiences. Identify your favorite personas and feel free to add to the list if you don't see your most prominent personas. As you read the descriptions you may notice that some of your prominent personas are flavored with aspects of others. For example, you may see that your Conscientious persona has Self-righteous overtones, or that your Devoted persona has a Caretaker edge. Do you best to discover the personas that show up most in your relationships, while noticing nuances.

Conscientious: These people go the extra mile, even if they don't feel like it. As children they would be the ones who supervised the cutting of the pie to make sure everyone got their fair share. Right and wrong are important concepts to Conscientious personas.
BUMPER STICKER: Do the right thing, or else.

Supercompetent: This persona specializes in handling the material world and organizational matters better than anyone else. Supercompetent children often have "a place for everything and everything in its place." Efficiency is an important concept to a Supercompetent.
BUMPER STICKER: Here, let me do it.

Devoted: If this persona were an animal, it would be a dog. Devoted personas are very loyal, uncritical of the chosen one(s), and can be counted on to remember occasions and anniversaries. As children, they aspired to always be loving and kind to everyone.
BUMPER STICKER: I'll always be here for you.

Drama Queen/King: Everything is a big deal. The Drama personas can stir up a tempest by walking into a room. When they were children, life may have appeared to be a "tempest in a teapot." The world occurs in extremes to and around this persona. Drama Queens and Kings speak in bold italics.
BUMPER STICKER: You would not *believe* the day I've had.

Ramblin' Guy/Gal: These personas place special value on expansion and the far-off horizon. They mistrust commitments as possible traps. Ramblin' children are off on adventures constantly and often can't be located for household chores. The possibility around the corner is an important concept to the Rambler.
BUMPER STICKER: Don't fence me in.

Victim: Bad things happen to these personas regularly. They are magnets for misery. They are convinced that it's not their fault and have difficulty discriminating fault from responsibility. When this persona begins to appear as a strategy in childhood, getting bullied, being picked last for teams, and being scapegoated may be factors.
BUMPER STICKER: Why Me?

Performer: Life is a stage for the performer, and s/he is always *on*. Communications are played to the back row. Developing Performers focus on the effect, whether they specialize as jokers, thespians, magicians, or poets.
BUMPER STICKER: The show must go on, wherever I go.

Critic: Discrimination and aesthetics are very important to the Critic. The Critic often fuses judgment with fault and looks for possible flaws in things and shortcomings in people. One Critic remembered, as a child, adjusting her mother's jewelry and makeup before letting her parent leave for a party.
BUMPER STICKER: I'll tell you what's wrong. Even if you don't ask.

Loner: This persona is prone to develop adoption and alien theories

about his/her childhood. "I was left here by beings from another galaxy," or "My real parents will come back for me after I've done my time in this awful family" are common Loner thoughts. This is the outsider, by choice. Loners may also feel superior to mere mortals.
BUMPER STICKER: By myself.

Space Out: These personas live more comfortably in a fantasy world than with the rigors of responsible adult life. Often forgetful, they have difficulty keeping time agreements. Favorite occupation is hanging out.
BUMPER STICKER: Huh?

Mr./Ms. Nice Guy: This is the tapioca of personas. Mr./Ms. Nice Guy is even-tempered and cheerful. Often overriding hostile impulses and eschewing selfish desires, the Nice Guys were often rewarded for social propriety as children. Told to "be nice," they were.
BUMPER STICKER: Aw, shucks!

Dependent/Clingy: The dependent persona definitely leans toward closeness to the detriment of his/her own autonomy. These personas keep an eye on the partner and have difficulty standing on their own two feet, figuring out what they want, and opposing the partner's decisions. Developing Dependents were often mamas' boys and daddies' girls.
BUMPER STICKER: But I need you!

Mr.Sick/Ms. Accidents: These related personas account for most of the medical costs in the emergency room. As children they learned to deal with stress and/or get attention by becoming accident prone or ill. Asking for what they want directly is often a problem. They may have special diets and rigid health regimes.
BUMPER STICKER: Whoops!

Caretaker: This persona will be the first to offer a tissue (not the box) to a crying person. The helpers and rescuers of the world,

they leap first and inquire later. As children, Caretakers may have been told something like, "I always know I can count on your help." Whole movements have developed recently to help people recover from this persona.
BUMPER STICKER: Let me help you.

Stoic: Maintenance of stone-faced perseverance in the face of obstacles is an important goal for the Stoic. Seemingly lacking emotions, Stoics often bury feelings under rigidity and ritual. "No pain, no gain" may be an important belief. On camping trips as children, they would be the ones who insisted that the best way to sleep is rolled up in a blanket on the ground.
BUMPER STICKER: I can take it.

Peter Pan/Tinker Bell: These personas can be very appealing and attractive. Youthful and effervescent, these are the perpetual youngsters of the world. They are often skillful at skirting responsibility in a way that the "grown-up" finds both charming and irritating. They are frequently attempting to outrun aging and responsibility.
BUMPER STICKER: I'll never grow up.

Hostile: The world is a bad place to this persona. You'd better get them before they get you is a common belief. Hostile personas would rather insult you than negotiate. Vulnerable and sad emotions are often buried under this mask of guardedness.
BUMPER STICKER: Out of my way, M______f______!

Self-righteous: This persona knows better, always, on any subject. People who have developed this persona often have "special" feelings. That is, they know that they don't have to follow the known laws of the universe because they're "special." In restaurants, they would be the ones to send dinner back with instructions for the chef.
BUMPER STICKER: Well! I never!

Chameleon: The masters of adaptation, Chameleons are perceptive and can adjust to changing situations and people easily and with

grace. Unfortunately, this flexibility is often at the cost of a solid center. Chameleons don't know who they are and have difficulty maintaining a steady sense of direction. Childhood may have been unpredictable, if relatively untroubled. Conflict is difficult for the Chameleon if a stand is called for.
BUMPER STICKER: Whatever you say!

True Believer: These personas are the foot soldiers and loyal yes-men of movements and organizations. They gravitate toward the security of dogma and rarely question authority or beliefs. As children, True Believers backed up the captains and ringleaders, echoing their taunts and challenges.
BUMPER STICKER: This is IT!

Shy: The world is a big, scary place to this persona. Shy personas may have a lot to say, but they usually keep it to themselves. As children they may have been the wallflowers or loners, or they may have compensated for their shyness by being invisible joiners.
BUMPER STICKER: I'll wait in the car.

Flamboyant: This persona is gregarious and pushes the edges of social conventions. Often loud in voice and dress, the Flamboyant persona looks for the newest trend and aspires to create one. As children, these personas were often too much for their parents and friends.
BUMPER STICKER: This is just the latest thing.

Martyr: Martyrs have perfected the art form of suffering and sacrificing for others. They tend to give by giving up their desires and giving over their power to others. As children, developing Martyrs were often rewarded for giving up what they really wanted to keep the peace or placate a parent.
BUMPER STICKER: No, you go ahead without me.

Delinquent/Rebel: These are the different ones. They go their own way, march to a different drummer, etc. The Rebel not only doesn't like to be told what to do, s/he will often defy authority reflexively.

Example: In the movie *The Wild One,* the older man asks Marlon Brando's character, "Say, what are you kids rebelling against, anyway?!" The response: "Whadda ya got?"
BUMPER STICKER: Not me, man.

STEP TWO:

Think about which of these personas are most prominent in your life. Do the same for your parents and anyone else who was significant in your upbringing. Choose a number from 1 to 10 that reflects the extent to which you and they wear each persona in relationships. There is space at the end to add personas that you don't see on the list. Participants have found it useful to go through the whole list. For example, one man said that he discovered overlapping patterns between his personas and those of his parents and grandparents that had been invisible to him when he just focused on one or two obvious personas.

1–2 = Almost never
3–4 = Seldom
5–6 = Sometimes
7–8 = A lot
9–10 = Almost always

PERSONA	ME	MOTHER	FATHER	OTHER SIGNIFICANT PERSON
Conscientious				
Supercompetent				
Devoted				
Drama Queen/King				
Ramblin' Guy/Gal				
Victim				

Performer
Critic
Loner
Space Out
Mr./Ms. Nice Guy
Dependent/Clingy
Mr. Sick/Ms. Acci-
dent
Caretaker
Stoic
Peter Pan/Tinker Bell
Hostile
Self-righteous
Chameleon
True Believer
Shy
Flamboyant
Martyr
Delinquent/Rebel
____
____
____

DISCUSSION:

As you study the columns of numbers, do you notice any themes or patterns? People have made surprising discoveries about the source of their personas. Look for extremes in agreement or disagreement between your numbers for each persona and those of significant others. Several people noticed they had learned not to compete with a parent's persona. If father was a 10 Conscientious, the son or daughter usually rated only 2 or 3. It can also be useful to look down the list for similar numbers among different personas. For example, one woman realized that her strong Supercompetent persona (9) developed in relation to her mother's equally strong (9) Martyr persona.

The Persona Interview

This partner activity has two purposes. One is to acknowledge and flesh out the conscious experience of a particular persona. When we recognize how much we have been run by various personas, the first impulse may be to try and perform a persona-ectomy. Even if this were possible, and it isn't, persona exploration can be useful and enlivening. Giving the persona a chance to speak directly can lead to an experience of the emotions and authentic expressions that personas mask. The other purpose of this activity is to give you more of a sense of the interplay between your personas and your partner's.

INSTRUCTIONS:

Decide who will be the first interviewer and who the first interviewee. The interviewee will pick a persona to explore. Take a moment to let yourself stand and think as this persona. When you are ready to be interviewed, take a giant step forward *into* the persona. Don't rehearse, just let this persona speak the first response that comes to mind.

Interviewer, when your partner steps into persona, ask the following questions. Be sure to address your partner as her/his persona at the beginning of each question (e.g., "Loner" . . . , not "Bob" . . .). You may think of other questions to add at the end. Use this as an outline. When you have finished the questions, take a moment to shake off your roles, then switch places. Feel free to interview more than one persona.

- "(Loner), what's the most important thing to you?"
- "________________, what are you most proud of?"
- "________________, when did you make your first appearance?"
- "________________, who did you learn your style from?"
- "________________, what are you most afraid of?"
- "________________, what do you most want?"

DISCUSSION:

Seminar and therapy participants have been amazed at the information stored by their personas and its ready emergence with just an invitation. We want to experience our personas fully and acknowledge all the ways they've served us. When appreciation rather than disapproval occurs, a persona's hard edges and defenses seem to melt magically, allowing it to embrace more of our essential characteristics. Also, couples have found that when they own their predominant personas, they don't seem to lock into the same conflicts with each other.

The Costs and Payoffs of Attachment to Personas

This activity is designed to explore a predominant persona in more depth. We have isolated the chief reasons that people continue to express persona rather than their essential selves long after the initial need for personas has passed. Choose a persona to work with and use it as you fill in the blanks in the following sentences.

When I'm in my ________________ persona,
I don't have to feel ________________, or ________________,
or ________________.

I get to be right and make ________________ wrong.

I get to control ________________.

I get to avoid being controlled by ________________.

But . . .

I don't get to try out the creative strategies of ________________,
or ________________, or ________________.

I lose vibrancy by ______________.

I don't make authentic contact with ______________.

I lose the opportunity for receiving ______________'s love.

Sometimes being in a particular persona requires others to be a certain way, that is, to assume a complementary role. (For example, a Supercompetent may require others to be lazy or ineffective so the Supercompetent can feel competent and in charge; a Ramblin' Guy/Gal may require a Dependent/Clingy partner to prove to the Ramblin' Guy/Gal that his/her emotional distancing is justified.)

My ______________ persona requires that ______________ be ______________.

DISCUSSION:

When couples discover that they have actually been *requiring* the most obnoxious traits in their partners, some laugh, some cry, but all are transformed by the awareness. For example, when the light bulb came on for one woman, she exclaimed, "You mean my Martyr persona actually requires that Todd ignore me and override my requests! I can't believe it—I *can* believe it! If he were nice to me, I wouldn't know what to do!"

Integrating Personas

This list suggests some attitudes and actions that various personas need to learn. Personas often mask developmental tasks that humans need to master to be whole. They also can mask feelings that need to be experienced for the persona to become an expression of our essential selves. Examine this list in light of the persona work you've already done. See if these tasks resonate with your persona's needs.

PERSONA	NEEDS TO LEARN HOW TO
Conscientious	relax, be okay with failure, lighten expectations of perfection in self and others
Supercompetent	empower others, delegate and follow up, cultivate inner stillness
Devoted	cultivate an inner life of one's own, be sensitive to own needs, establish boundaries
Drama Queen/King Performer/Flamboyant	meditate, develop inner quiet; know that self is loved for self and not only for performance
Ramblin' Guy/Gal	be close without running, set boundaries so self is not engulfed
Victim	take responsibility for own life, express anger without blame, forgive
Critic	love self unconditionally, forgive and separate from parents
Loner	reach out, share feelings with others, acknowledge pain
Space Out	stay with body sensations and get results
Mr./Ms. Nice Guy	be angry effectively, say no, own shadow feelings
Dependent/Clingy	make own decisions, separate own experience from others', consciously ask for help instead of unconsciously demanding/expecting it

Mr. Sick/Ms. Accidents	identify and express feelings on the spot, ask for nurturing consciously
Caretaker	get others to take responsibility, let self be taken care of; discover that self can be loved without being useful
Stoic	acknowledge vulnerability, loosen up, feel emotions and sensations
Peter Pan/Tinker Bell	keep agreements, follow through on responsibilities, grow up
Hostile/Rebel	listen to others, focus on getting ahead rather than getting even, acknowledge and love inadequacies in self rather than covering with bluster
Self-righteous	get unstuck from positions gracefully, make amends, apologize, feel lovable even when wrong or committing errors
Chameleon	acknowledge own wants and feelings, take space consciously, cultivate steadiness and clarity through meditation and telling truth
True Believer	question, listen to own experience, value self, forgive and separate from parents
Shy	take graduated risks, speak out, speak up; discover that self can be loved when not hiding
Martyr	avoid making suffering right, enjoy enjoyment, make friends with own body

DISCUSSION:

After looking over this list, decide which persona you would be willing to focus on for the next month as an ongoing project. Some of the tasks can be implemented immediately, and some will take time to develop and master. When you have decided, make a list of steps you will take to learn those persona tasks, and when. If you find yourself changing priorities and developing new tasks, alter your list. We recommend reviewing your persona work once a week until it becomes integrated into your daily life.

Example:

PERSONA	TASK	ACTION	WHEN
Chameleon	acknowledging own wants and feelings	ask, "What do I want?" (start with daily decisions like food, clothes, schedules, going out)	daily
		ask, "What are my body sensations and emotions?"	every hour (set watch)
	taking space	take time off for no good reason	once/week
	cultivating steadiness	initiate alone time, meditation time	daily
	cultivating clarity	explore communication activities until truth is recognizable and easy to communicate	once/week

Use the following chart to outline your persona work.

PERSONA	TASK	ACTION	WHEN

EXERCISES ON PROJECTIONS

In the years since we wrote *Centering and the Art of Intimacy* we have come to appreciate and respect the enormous power of projection. We often tell couples that if they solve this central problem it will transform the quality of their relationship beyond their wildest imaginings. Projection is the central hook that snatches couples from intimacy into the quagmire of power struggles. When a person exclaims indignantly, "But, wait a minute, s/he really does ________." we know we're witnessing the hook.

Getting people to recognize and transform projection calls for skillful noticing and intervention. Most people really resist turning the pointed finger of projection toward themselves. And these are people who have some investment, both monetary and time, in clearing up projection. It is an enormous act of courage to wrestle our projections into clarity. It is also the most effective and powerful move we can make.

The following experiences are reliable indicators of projection. In your explorations notice when you feel:

- righteous
- indignant
- wronged
- blameless
- in a life-or-death struggle
- absolutely certain that it's your partner's fault

We can say with certainty, after working with over a thousand couples, projection is the central energy drain in entangled relationships. And most couples come in fighting over whose projection it is, or whose fault it is. To repeat a very important sentence from *Centering and the Art of Intimacy:* "You get to know what's projection and what's not only after you're willing to consider everything as a projection." Many couples start sputtering in aggrieved tones when we suggest exploring everything as a possible projection. But it is a simple solution, and it works. Projection can be transformed into creative intimacy instantly by considering this central question: *"What might this issue have to do with me?"* If you ask and meditate on this question alone, in every situation, over the next few months, you will take the most powerful step possible to heal yourself and your relationship.

The following activities are refinements of this central question that may be useful as you work through projection.

Journal Activity

On a fresh left-hand page in your journal, fill in the blanks in the following sentences. Ask yourself, *"What is it about my partner that drives me nuts?"*

- S/he's way too ________________.
- S/he's not ________________ enough.
- S/he's really lacking in ________________.
- S/he always ________________.
- If s/he would only ________________.
- I can't believe s/he ________________again.

Now, on the opposite page, take each sentence and ask, *"What might this issue have to do with me?"*

Notice your thoughts and feelings as you ask this question. We've found that anger is a sure sign that projection is involved. Give yourself permission to experience your feelings and continue to ask what this issue might have to do with you. Even if your responses seem farfetched, acknowledge your intention to reclaim and own the hook of projection.

Example:

- S/he's way too bossy.
- S/he's not sexy enough.
- S/he's really lacking in articulateness.
- S/he always corrects me in public.
- If s/he would only clean up after cooking.
- I can't believe s/he overdrew the checking account again.

- What might *bossy* have to do with me? I don't see myself as bossy. But I get upset if everything isn't straightened up before we go out or do something fun.
- What might *not sexy* enough have to do with me? I remember in high school the guys who had really sexy girlfriends were cooler than us brainier types who had few dates at all, much less with sexy girls. I guess I've thought that if you love me, a nerd, you must not be sexy enough.
- What might a *lack of articulateness* have to do with me? Well, I'm really sharp about fixing things and talking about the logic of a situation. But when it comes to feelings, whew, I just get tongue-tied.
- What might *correcting in public* have to do with me? This one's a hard one to face. Let's see . . . I realize that Doris has been trying to get me to be more social when she reminds me of people's names when we're out. And I get embarrassed that I've forgotten, so I pick on her grammar. Ugh.
- What might *cleaning up after cooking* have to do with me? I think I may have a double standard here. When Doris cooks, I see that as her job, and the job isn't finished until the kitchen is clean. But on the rare occasions when I make something or get a snack, I don't think I'm really *doing* anything, so I don't clean up.
- What might *overdrawing the checking account* have to do with me? This is the main place we have power struggles, over money. I make the money, so I have the major responsibility to see that there's enough for all our bills, funds, savings, and so on. Maybe Doris feels left out of this process. I'll have to ask her if she's angry about how we handle our money—probably is.

When each of you has completed the entire activity, share your discoveries with each other. Many couples find that this exercise opens surprisingly helpful perspectives and possibilities for ending power struggles.

Who Is Seeing?

This activity is designed to clarify and open your perspective. Projection is literally an out-of-body experience. We often use the analogy of a movie projector when explaining the process of projection. The images on the screen are so compelling that very few people in the audience spend their time gazing back at the projector in the far wall. But the projector is the source of the pictures. Similarly, when we look at our partner, we forget that we are the source of how we see.

INSTRUCTIONS:

You'll need a tape recorder with a microphone that you can read the following questions and sentences into. Read each sentence slowly and pause for two long, slow breaths before moving to the next. Don't worry about responding verbally; just notice your reaction to these questions.

- What thoughts and body sensations come up for you as you look at your partner?
- Who is the you who is seeing this person?
- Is it more important to be right than it is to see the essence of this person?
- When did I first learn to see the world this way?
- Be aware of whatever your body and mind are doing.
- Notice this face carefully. Is this the face you'd want to be looking at as you say good-bye to this life?
- Through the eyes you're seeing through, is there space for this person to be magnificent? To be okay?
- In the quality of your seeing and listening, is there space for your partner to reach her/his full evolution?
- Does your seeing or listening hold your partner back at all?
- Does your seeing or listening make space for celebration?

When you are ready, sit facing each other, with or without touch contact as you prefer, and stay in eye contact as you listen to the words you've recorded. After the tape is finished, rest for a few minutes. First record your discoveries in your journal, then take a few minutes to share whatever you've learned with your partner.

The Projection Theater

In these sentence-completion activities you'll get a chance to connect your favorite projections with the actions they produce. Our projections have tremendous impact on the ways we interact with our partners and the world. It's very tempting to point the finger and say, "It's your fault." It's much more difficult and more empowering to claim our responsibility in creating our world.

Take a blank sheet in your journal and complete the following sentences. You may wish to complete some more than once as you uncover more attitudes and projections.

- In order to see the world as ________________, I must be ________________.

(e.g., In order to see the world as making me wrong, I must be feeling not good enough. In order to see the world as a hostile place, I must be feeling scared.)

- If I am acting ________________, the world (other people) looks ________________.

(e.g., If I am acting supercompetent, the world looks incompetent. If I am acting dependent, other people look strong and dependable. If I am acting like a loner, other people look intrusive and clingy.)

- In order to see my partner as ________________, I must be ________________.

(e.g., In order to see my partner as a policeman, I must be a rebel. In order to see my partner as inferior, I must be superior.)

- If I am acting ________________, my partner looks _____.

(e.g., If I am acting like a victim, my partner looks like my oppressor. If I am acting like a critic, my partner looks like s/he's doing it wrong.)

- If ____________________really looks like it's my partner's fault, I must be seeing ___________________.

(e.g., If the mess around here really looks like it's my partner's fault, I must be seeing our house as only her/his responsibility. If our arguments look like my partner's fault, I must be seeing that I'm right.)

Moving Through Projection

For this activity, use a tape recorder or camcorder to record your responses so you'll be free to experiment without focusing on remembering what you said.

STEP ONE

Start about 10 feet apart. Partner A moves away from Partner B until s/he notices a thought, body sensation, or internal visual image *about* Partner B. Partner A then reports the experience out loud. Partner A then moves closer to Partner B until s/he notices a thought, body sensation, or internal visual image *about* Partner B, then stops to report it out loud.
Repeat these steps four or five times, then switch roles.

Example:

- Sheila moves a few steps away from Cameron. "You look angry."
- Sheila then moves closer to Cameron until she notices an experience. "I had a thought that you must be bored with me."
- Moving away again: "Your shoulders are tensing up."
- Moving closer: "You look smaller as I get closer."

STEP TWO

Each partner write a list of what you said (and did) in a column on the left side of a large piece of paper. When the list is complete, move to the right side of the page and rewrite each sentence beginning with "I . . ." or "My . . ."

Example:

You look angry.	I am feeling irritated today.
You must be bored with me.	I am bored with me.
Your shoulders are tensing up.	My shoulders and neck are tensing up.
You look smaller as I get closer.	I get smaller when I get close to you.

Are any of your "I/My . . ." sentences familiar? Are things you criticized in your partner or have been criticized for yourself experiences in common? Explore together how what you see might be a mirror of who you are.

Open yourself up to the possibility that what you think is about your partner may be an unclaimed part of yourself. Are there any commitments or actions that will support each of you in claiming these unowned aspects of yourselves? For example, one couple went on a "you" diet. They practiced communicating only with sentences that began with "I." They were astounded to discover how difficult it was to stay with "I" and how tempting it was to move into "you." After a week or so they noticed that they were each experiencing more intimacy *and* more creativity. Their usual round of complaints had largely disappeared.

PROBLEM SOLVING

After twenty-plus years of work with couples, we have confirmed two central truths:

1. You are never upset for the reason you think.
2. Problems aren't solved in the state of awareness in which they occur.

For example, in a couples session recently, the wife was complaining about her husband's lack of responsibility. "If only he would contribute his fair share in daily tasks I could get some rest and not feel overwhelmed all the time!" He looked rather sheepish, but defiant, as she exclaimed about his regular shortcomings in the duty arena. As we worked with the couple, using the key instructions you'll be practicing in a moment, they discovered that the ongoing argument always occurred when they had the opportunity for some unstructured play time. She began to realize that she had no idea how to receive nurturing from her husband. Her early family experience had been isolated and chaotic, so she learned to take care of herself (and everything else) before she entered school. In other words, she was a responsibility policeman. He began to see that he had learned to be oppositional in his relationship with his father. Being a delinquent was the only way to get his father's attention. So he needed a policeman in order to relate at all. They began to see that they were not only stuck in a pattern but glued to a constant repetition of strategies that had been devised by children.

This activity creates space for truth to emerge magically and for solutions to spontaneously flower from the creative storehouse waiting to be unlocked by willingness and openness. The structure is very simple; the results can be profound.

INSTRUCTIONS:

Stand facing your partner. Have a Ping-Pong communication exchange, where you take turns saying out loud, *"I am willing to solve the problem."* Pause after each statement for two deep, relaxed belly breaths. Notice whatever sensations, emotions, and specific thoughts arise during the pause. Each of you says the phrase out loud four or five times.

Now take turns saying the phrase out loud, pausing for two long breaths, and telling the truth about whatever you experience. Do your best to just notice and describe; avoid analysis.

Example:

Fred: I am willing to solve the problem. [*pause*] I notice my shoulders hitching up and the thought, Yeah, right, I wish it was that simple!

Gloria: I am willing to solve the problem. [*pause*] I feel really confused and sad. I don't really know what the problem is.

Fred: I am willing to solve the problem. [*pause*] I notice a little sense of lightness in my chest, and you look different to me than you did a few minutes ago. That's really interesting! You seem more friendly, prettier. I wonder if I have anything to do with that.

Gloria: I am willing to solve the problem. [*pause*] I felt a breeze of relief through my front. I really am willing to solve the problem; it's not just words. And I still don't understand, but I feel clearer inside.

Learning to Love Yourselves Together

Most problems in relationships are a reflection of feeling unlovable. In the perfect fit that most couples have, one person's unlovable feelings trigger a complementary set in his/her partner, and off they go, fighting for the victim position. Instead of defending or denying these natural feelings, we suggest learning to love these states in each other. The following exercise is best done at a quiet, uninterrupted time.

INSTRUCTIONS:

Decide who will be the first lover and who the lovee. Lovee, identify the place in your body that gets tense, tight, or painful when you feel unlovable. Lover, hold that place and love your partner's essence.

Lovee, while the lover is holding you, tell the truth about all the emotions, sensations, images, and thoughts connected with feeling unlovable. Keep saying out loud whatever emerges as you focus on the experience of feeling unlovable.

Lover, keep holding, and, lovee, keep telling the truth until you feel complete. This will be signaled by feeling blissful, peaceful, and/or lovable. After a pause, switch roles.

Becoming Aware of Your Underlying Intentions

Many problems in relationships are not caused by what we say but how we say it. Research indicates that upward of 80 percent of communication is nonverbal. So it's often not the content that causes uproar, but the sighs, inflections, body language, and accompanying symphony of nonverbal communication that is the culprit. Awareness is a powerful tool in fitting your communication more closely to your experience. Use this activity to check your communication intentions and see if you want to revise your attitudes or actions.

INSTRUCTIONS:

Each of you write down your account of your last argument, from beginning to end. First, what did you say and what did your partner say? What happened, what did you see, feel, and notice? Do your best to not edit.

Working independently from your partner, look at each of the following questions and use it to examine your account of the argument.

- *Did what and how you communicated produce the result you intended?* For example, did you intend to create a unified plan to deal with the kids' homework, and instead, the result produced by your communication is that your partner is sleeping in the living room? Here is the bottom line. The result you create reflects your unconscious intention.
- *Why did this argument arise at this time?* In other words, what might be happening between you and your partner if you weren't engaged in this conflict? Couples find that these questions uncover the potential that conflict often overshadows. For example, opportunities to have spontaneous fun get overrun by habitual power struggles.
- *What is the truth about your communication?* What's the deepest, unarguable truth? Go back over your account of the argument and search for the sentences that couldn't possibly be argued about. You may not find any. If not, look inside to discover the truth that you want to communicate. We may say, for example, "I didn't mean to start an argument." But the result is that an argument ensued. Recognize that the result is your unconscious intention and tell the truth about it. "I don't want to argue and I do want to argue." That asserts your responsibility again and allows you to create clearly what you most deeply want.

After you have completed these questions, share your discoveries with each other. What did you learn about *your* communication style? Is there anything you want to make new agreements about?

The Delicate Art of Giving Feedback

What distinguishes feedback from criticism? In our explorations with couples and colleagues we have come to see that for most people the distinction between giving genuine feedback and criticizing is quite muddied. People confuse control and blame with feedback. Very few people see when they are projecting instead of giving feedback. And often opinions and judgments are disguised as feedback, creating confusion and misunderstanding.

One of the first communication errors that many partners make is to give unsolicited feedback. Take a moment and reflect on your agreements with your partner. Have you consciously decided that your relationship is transparent, that each of you is deeply interested in growth? Is each of you more interested in growth or in looking good? In our book *Conscious Loving* we discuss this in the Six Co-commitments as "I commit to revealing rather than concealing." Over the years we've found that this commitment is the most difficult for most people. So many of us associate revealing ourselves with pain and hurt, and it seems crazy to voluntarily open ourselves to more. We have found that truth is the only safety, the unarguable truth. If your relationship is grounded in the commitment to telling the truth, everything that comes up can become fuel for intimacy and growth.

The agreement to welcome feedback can be one of the liveliest couples make, but making an unconscious deal to keep an eye on the other is very different and creates dramatically different results. For example, several years ago I (Kathlyn) was focusing on dressing to enhance my features. I asked Gay to give me feedback if something I was wearing didn't look good on me. One Sunday as we were dressing to present a lecture, he said, "That dress makes you look fat." My first response was hurt and outrage. What poor timing! Didn't he see I was gearing up to be in public and didn't need to be undercut at the last minute?! After a few heated moments I remembered that I had *asked* Gay for feedback. Here I had responded to him much the same way the Terri Garr character responded in the movie *Tootsie* when Dustin Hoffman told her the truth about being in love with another woman. "I know I asked, I just didn't know how I would *feel* about it!" she sputtered after she exploded at him.

Feedback can bring up deep feelings and memories. Gay's feedback brought up years of sadness over feeling plump and unattractive, as well as anger that I first directed at him. I, as do most people, heard his words as, "There's something wrong with you." Fortunately, I soon remembered my commitment to revealing. I really did want to know anything that prevented me from being as effective as possible. As I explored my feelings, I found that I had been a little unsure of my presentation that day; I didn't feel like a shining example of enlightened couplehood. I realized I had unconsciously dressed to match that internal state, which Gay had seen and reflected back to me. I changed my outfit and donated the other one.

In this activity you'll learn to give and receive feedback in a neutral way. Most couples find this process very rewarding, even in the initial stages.

STEP ONE

The Contract

Make an agreement with your partner about your availability for feedback. Are you open to feedback all the time? Do you want to be asked first, "Do you want feedback about this?" Would it be most empowering for each of you to ask for feedback rather than wait for it? Take some time to decide what your intention is here and make an agreement that works for both of you. Many people find that asking is very helpful as they sort out their past experiences of criticism from the present intention to receive feedback. When you have made an agreement, write it down and put it somewhere visible, like on the bathroom mirror or the refrigerator.

STEP TWO

Practicing Description

It is useful to pretend you are speaking to a Martian in this activity. Assume that your partner doesn't know your personal shorthand, idioms, or clichés. We'll focus on the meaning of *describe* given in the dictionary: "to trace or outline." Rather than interpreting and judging, do your best to outline what you see and experience.

Stand facing each other. Decide who will be the first subject and who the first describer. Subject, make a face. Choose any expression you wish, and hold that face for a minute or so. Describer, verbally describe what you see. How is the subject's face shaped? What parts stand out? Do your best to paint such a vivid picture that someone hearing your words in another room could draw a picture that matches the face your partner is making.

When the description is complete, switch roles. Each of you make three or four faces and describe them.

The following two examples are included to help you distinguish between description and interpretation.

Description: "I see your eyebrows scrunched toward the middle of your face, and there are two deep vertical furrows between your eyebrows. Your eyes are almost closed. Your nose has wrinkles along the sides, and the tip is drawn up. Your mouth is puckered with a circle opening about the size of a dime. Your chin has little indentations in it, and your cheeks under your cheekbones are hollowed out, a little more on the left than the right."

Interpretation: "You look like you're smelling something bad, or like you're angry. I think you're angry with me and won't tell me."

Now decide who will be the first talker and who the first describer. Talker, take several minutes to discuss an issue you're working on or a problem you want to solve. Describer, watch and listen as your partner speaks. When s/he is finished, reflect back to the talker what you saw and heard as if you were mirroring exactly what happened. Of course you'll tend to want to color your account with projections and interpretations, but do your best to reflect. When you are finished, switch roles. Only after each of you has had a turn, discuss your experiences when being described.

STEP THREE

Practicing Owning Your Experience

Stand or sit facing each other and maintain eye contact. Choose a recent issue or problem *that you are both willing to solve.* Take turns exchanging sentences about your experience. The key in this step is "I." Begin all your sentences with "I," rather than "you." Continue exchanging "I" sentences until the issue shifts.

Example:
Keri: I'm confused and don't know what to do.
Daniel: I feel my mind going blank.
Keri: I want more help with the household stuff.
Daniel: I feel pushed when you say that.
Keri: I'm scared to ask you for things.
Daniel: You look scared . . . no, wait . . . I'm experiencing hesitation and a kind of shutting down.
Keri: I just had an image of my father and mother after dinner, when my dad would go into the den and read the paper, while my mother would bang pots and pans around but not ask for dad's help with the dishes. I remember that whenever she did ask, he'd roar about how hard he worked all day.
Daniel: I feel my chest letting go with a whoosh. I'm relieved to hear your memory. I've been afraid that all my free time will be taken up with chores. I am willing to help.

Interrupting Routines

Being close observers of the cycles of relationship, we have cataloged some sure signs of the deadly routine monster. When we're in a restaurant and see a couple who are both looking into the middle distance with rather blank expressions, we tend to think, "long-term, boring marriage." We don't tend to think that of a couple who are holding hands, smiling, and talking with animation. We think, rather, "humm, dating. She hasn't snagged him yet."

It's a shame, really, that we tend to see routine as synonymous with relationship. Many articles in women's magazines (note the role of responsibility here) discuss ways to revive your man's interest in the relationship when the inevitable doldrums occur. We advocate an equally shared responsibility for re-creating your bond and interest in growth. One of the most effective methods for maintaining interest is jostling set patterns.

INSTRUCTIONS:

The following are some simple and effective methods for interrupting routines and opening new possibilities for contact. Couples who have used them find them especially helpful when they are stuck.

- *Have a writing conversation (no talking), with each of you using your nondominant hand.* We recommend using a large sheet of blank paper for this activity and having oil pastels in a variety of colors on hand. Couples discover the process of their communication using this technique, rather than getting bogged down in the content. For example, one pair discovered that she interrupted just before he completed a sentence. Another couple noticed that they were very careful to define how much of the paper was "theirs." Each was waiting for the other to "cross the line."
- *If you enjoy the writing conversation, try a drawing conversation, with no words on the paper.* Couples have found they quickly come to the core of their issue using this activity, and it tends to soften the hard edges that often come with habitual verbal patterns.
- *Move and speak at the same time.* Often in stress we freeze in a position or belief that keeps us recycling the same pattern with each other. Find the place in your body that is most frozen and gently move it as you speak.
- *Drop the words and have a nonverbal conversation.* We have worked with many couples who get locked into verbal analysis and interpretation with an intensity that depletes any other kind of contact. They are amazed at the effect of dropping out the words and continuing communication with gestures and movement. A

new world of possibilities opens up. Sometimes couples will drop the words and continue the conversation with sounds and movement, with hilarious and lightening impact on the previously somber discussion.

- *Change positions as you speak*. For example, move your hands and arms into a new position, or stretch. If you feel adventurous, talk leaning over with your head between your legs or walk backward. Many people have noticed that they habitually sit in the same chair in the dining room, for example. At dinnertime, that place becomes associated over time with a certain personality and way of seeing partner and family. Gently interrupting positions can loosen stuck patterns in a way that partners find fun and even amusing.
- *Change places in the room with your partner*. Exchange places and sit or stand the way your partner was.
- *Exaggerate your position until it breaks down or shifts*. For example, if you are shaking your finger at your partner, keep shaking it more and more vigorously. One woman collapsed laughing as she felt the ridiculousness of her exaggerated pointing behavior. She said she felt like a hunting dog.

Choosing Relationship

We want to share with you the further reaches of intimacy. Beyond healing past wounds and making agreements that move into a new future, we want to propose a new context for relationship. Close relationship is about supporting and enhancing each other's highest potential. We think this is a better idea than using the relationship to comfortably snooze through life, or leaning on each other and limiting growth, or desperately holding on to positions for decades.

The central foundation for supporting each other's full potential is choosing the relationship. Choosing is an act of expanding, of coming forward into space rather than contracting and shrinking away. Choosing creates a boundary where both partners can be in touch with themselves *and* each other. For example: If I choose to tell the truth, to initiate speaking of a feeling I'm having, or a perception, I occupy space and present a tangible boundary for my partner to contact. If I have a feeling and conceal it, I contract into isolated space, out of contact with my partner. The incomplete feeling creates a vacuum. In the attempt to regain contact, my partner may be drawn to question, nag, or attack.

The consistent act of choosing experience is like using your energy to fill your own sails. The momentum carries you forward into the unknown waters of creativity in ways that may not initially be clear. New ideas pop up, seemingly out of nowhere. Connections between apparently unrelated things occur. Dreams become richer. Life changes from defending against the anticipated assault to welcoming the next opportunity to learn and create.

In each successful relationship we've encountered, at some point the partners actively and freely chose the relationship over a host of alternatives. And, sadly, we have also seen relationships in which people would rather die than give up a belief or pattern. Couples have also said, "I really want this relationship to work, but I'm just stuck. I don't understand why this keeps happening."

CONTACT

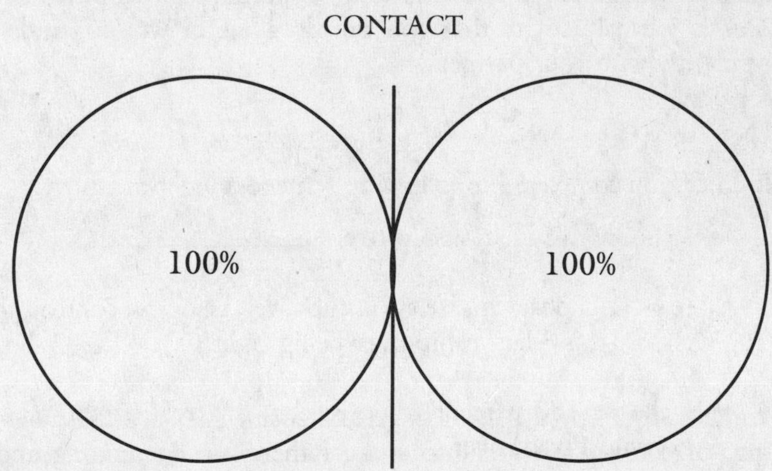

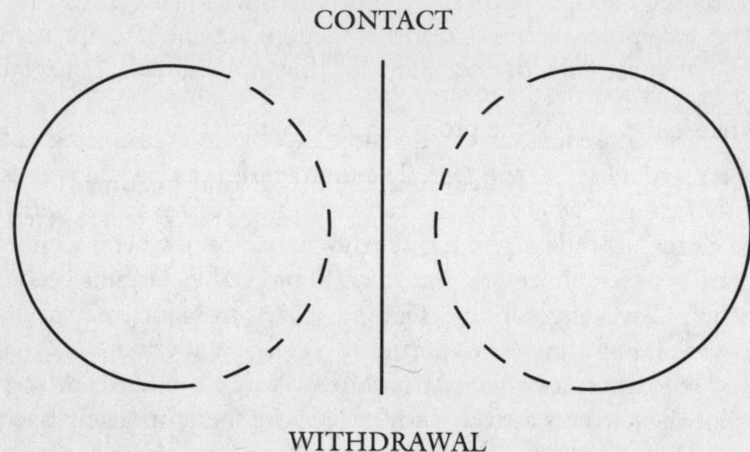

In times of conflict, the following activity can assist you in recognizing the thoughts and patterns that most often keep people stuck. This is journal activity that you can do alone or working independently with your partner.

INSTRUCTIONS:

Each of you complete the following sentences independently.

- I choose this relationship over __________________.

  (e.g., I choose this relationship over being in control; I choose this relationship over being right.)

- I choose 100 percent responsibility for creating the relationship I want over __________________.

  (e.g., waiting to respond to my partner's ideas; fighting over the scarcity of resources I imagine.)

- I choose to support my partner's potential over ________.

  (e.g., looking good; my timetable.)

Now do your best to summarize in one or two sentences and list in your journal the recurring conflict(s) of your relationship(s). What is the core of the problem? For example:

- John doesn't help around the house (and I get mad).
- Margaret flirts with everyone at parties (and I feel rejected).
- We don't talk enough.
- I can't stand his parents.
- We fight over how to raise the kids.

Next, look over the following list and ask, "Which of these am I choosing over making our relationship my absolute priority?' In other words, I prefer this way of being to having a relationship that works.

- I would rather be right.
- I prefer to be in control.
- I don't like people telling me what to do.
- I'm still mad about ________________, and I prefer to hold on to that.
- I learned ________________ from my parents, and that's the way I'm going to continue to be.
- I'm waiting for him/her to make the first move.

When you've looked carefully at your conflict and what you are currently choosing, ask yourself, "Am I willing to choose the relationship over ________________?" Notice what thoughts and feelings arise when you ask this question. Here are some examples of frequently encountered problematic responses.

- Now I have to do everything.
- If I do that, it will be all my fault.
- I want ________________ to admit fault.
- I don't know how else to be.
- I don't think it will do any good.

Whatever your response is, take two or three deep, long breaths to acknowledge and be with it, then ask again, "Am I willing to choose the relationship over ________________?" Stay with the process of asking and noticing until you can answer with a clear yes, or a clear no. Sometimes people are alarmed to discover that they are really not willing. A clear no, however, can unwind an entanglement as well as a clear yes. It gives you a ground to build on. Feelings and other ramifications result from "no," but "yes" also shifts the relationship in ways that bring up feelings and the need for new actions and agreements.

If you are doing this activity with a partner, continue with this last step. When each of you has completed the activity to this point, share your discoveries with the intention of noticing if any new agreements need to be made as a result of your exploration. Use your journals to note down the specific intentions and actions that you will make and take, and when.

Strategies for Getting Unstuck

Even the most enlightened couples get stuck now and then. The best intentions and most diligent integrity don't always prevent the demons from coming up. In fact, the love of a close relationship will invite the shadows and muck into the light where you can love and resolve them.

When people are stuck in their relationships, they often use the following words to describe their experience: stuck, solid, hard, heavy, dull, flat. These expressions have a similar quality of increased density and less liveliness. Regardless of the content, being stuck slows us down. If some action or movement can be generated in the stuck state, the relationship begins to look possible again. We seem to find solutions to insoluble problems without much effort. It's that first step that people find so difficult.

These strategies are designed to be used when you are stuck. They are tried and tested first steps to unsticking the problem. Most people find it useful to become familiar with them in a time of relative ease and harmony so the activities are easy to implement even when you feel hopeless.

- Take a few deep belly breaths and breathe out with a sound.
- Look around the room and describe what you actually see. Then look at your partner and describe what you see.
- Tell the truth. *Anything* that couldn't be argued about. For example, "My shoelace is untied. I see light on the desk. My throat is dry." Gay calls this "the cosmic steam iron."
- Say out loud, "I love myself for feeling ______________." Or "I love myself for being stuck."
- Move your body. Find the places that are tense and move them in a new way.
- Do something for someone else. This will often break the vapor lock of stuckness and restart the flow of positive energy.
- Express an appreciation about your partner. Find something that you are grateful for and say it out loud.

Creating a New Future

Most problem solving is mistakenly rooted in the past. We try to walk into the future looking over our shoulder at the way we've always done it. Or we are keeping score of our partner's faults or misdemeanors. The worst way to build your relationship is from the past. For those of you who have seen the movie *Scrooged,* or read Dickens's *A Christmas Carol,* problem solving from the past is like the chains on Marley's ghost. Each past slight or wrongdoing drags you down into the past again.

This activity gives you the opportunity to create a fresh future. You can design a future that will support new actions. Couples use this activity to form a future based on what they want rather than what they had. It is an extension of "The Enlightening Relationship Two-Step," an activity described earlier, with a problem-solving focus.

You will need enough clear space to stand and move around a little.

STEP ONE

Choose an issue that you are both interested in redesigning. Then decide who will be the creator first, and who will be the recorder. Recorder, you'll jot down the creator's words and actions during this part of the activity.

Creator, find a place in the room to stand that represents how it is. Take several minutes to fully communicate verbally and physically the truth about how it is. Include your perceptions, beliefs, projections, what you've learned, rules, feelings, body sensations, and anything else you notice. Explain how it is as if you were talking to a Martian who doesn't understand clichés, assumptions or the phrase "you know."

When you feel complete, switch roles.

STEP TWO

Creator, move to a new place in the room that represents the future. Actually step into the future, then turn to face your partner. From this place, standing in the future, describe what you want. Don't worry about *how* you're going to get there. Describe what you want as if it already exists. Paint it in as much detail as you wish. When you feel complete, switch roles. For example, this couple chose to work with the issue of better sex in their relationship.

HOW IT IS:

Myra: We seem to always have sex at the end of the day after work, kids, laundry, meals, ironing, etc. Often I'm just too tired. Then, I'm afraid I'm too fat and that you find me unattractive. Sex feels routine, like we're going through the motions. I find myself making lists during sex, and I'm embarrassed to admit that. I don't feel comfortable to tell you what I want. I learned that good girls didn't even think about sex, much less talk about it in detail. I know you get those magazines and hide them, but I sneak looks at the women; then I really feel dumpy.

Ned: My mind is on keeping my job right now, and I have a lot of anxiety about making ends meet, with the kids getting ready for high school, driving—college is just down the road. It seems like I don't have much juice left over for sex. I love you, but sex isn't very exciting anymore. It's interesting, I realize I learned that nice girls don't *have* sex either, so if sex were to be really great, I probably wouldn't respect you. Isn't that crazy!? . . . Women are still mysterious to me. I guess you're still mysterious to me. I don't know what you want, and sometimes I feel like it's all my job to please you, figure out what you need, run that whole show. Part of me just says, "Why bother."

WHAT I WANT (*From new places in the room*):

Myra: As if it already exists? . . . Okay. We make love at different times of the day, and in different rooms. Sometimes we tease each other about what we're going to do later. You call me from work and tell me you've been thinking about how much you like my skin and the way I smell. I tell you the things I like and appreciate you for being interested in pleasing me. I focus sometimes just on pleasuring you and don't let you do anything.

Ned: I'm liking this already. Let's see . . . We make a special date one evening a week, where no chores get done. We spend time doing something special together, dinner or a concert or a late picnic. The kids are banished to the movies or friends' houses. We spend at least an hour in foreplay, where we invent at least one new activity or variation and enjoy the favorites we've learned about. We feel easy about telling each other what we want and in exchanging roles to be receptive and active.

Gee, when can we start?

DISCUSSION:

You can use this activity for big or little issues in your relationship. Couples have found it especially useful with issues about sex and money. We chose sex as the example because that is one of the main areas of conflict and confusion in many relationships. Notice in the example that no time is spent justifying or explaining how it is or blaming the partner for the couple's experience. Also, the future doesn't have to bear much resemblance to how it is currently. You can make it up from this moment forward. After moving through this activity people notice a remarkable new space for resolution. Things seem to shift almost magically, without a lot of effort or struggle. When you have communicated the past and present completely, it is easier to release yourselves into a possible future that you design.

TAMING YOUR UPPER-LIMITS DRAGON

In *Centering and the Art of Intimacy* we spent a chapter discussing the upper-limits problem, which we now abbreviate to ULP, which resembles the sound some people make when they realize they've stumbled into another pattern of limiting positive energy. Since that book was published we have come to see that ULP is really

THE UPPER LIMITS DRAGON

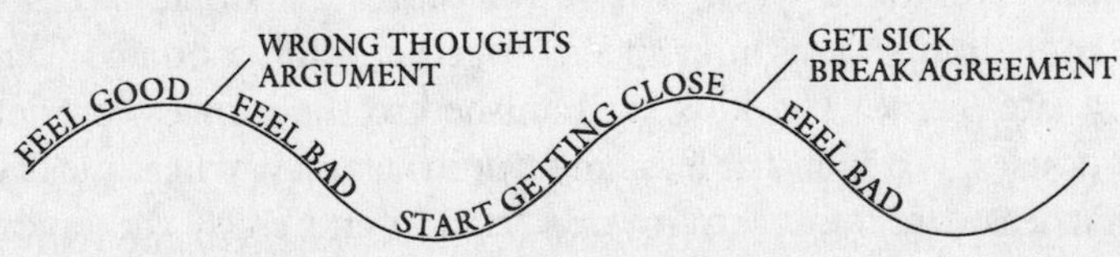

our basic relationship problem and evolutionary question. If we can spot the times and ways in which we automatically decrease our potential for more aliveness, we are charting new territory in human history. As a species we have thousands of years of experience in anticipating the worst and preparing for it. We have relatively little history where positive feelings such as love and harmony have been recognized, much less cultivated.

In close relationships, there is ultimately only one problem we need to solve: how not to place an upper limit on how much love and positive energy we exchange. When you open up to more love and energy, you begin to flush old glitches out of the system. Your energy thermostat is reset higher, and sometimes this sets off your alarms. Genuine contact with another person gets you high, and this trips the upper-limits switch, making you want to come back down to a more familiar level. We call this the upper-limits problem.

The alternative to setting upper limits is to notice when you are starting to get into something negative, recognize it as an upper-limits issue, and take steps to correct it. Some of the best steps are to feel the feelings in your body rather than projecting them onto someone else, tell the truth, take some space, breathe, love yourself.

There are several ways we limit positive energy in relationships. See if any of these are familiar. One is by starting arguments, out of fear of intimacy, at times when we could be exchanging intimacy. Another is by withholding significant communications. We get scared of being close, for example, and instead of telling the microscopic truth about it ("My belly felt tight and my skin contracted . . ."), we withdraw and swallow the communication. Another way we limit positive energy is by needing to control or dominate the other person (or needing to be controlled or dominated). If we always have to be right, for example, there is no room in the relationship for happiness and cocreativity.

After sorting out communication problems and the presenting issues that bring them into therapy, most couples come to realize that they repeat the upper-limits problem over and over. Then they feel better individually and together, that trips their energy thermostat, and ULP results. If you had to choose just one concept in this book to focus on, we'd recommend this series. If you can illuminate your particular ULP your life and relationship will take a giant leap.

Our explorations and research indicate that times of intimacy are the most common times for the upper-limits dragon to emerge. When you feel closest the temptation to control or slip into unconscious patterns will be strongest. These activities are designed to help you become aware of your upper-limits habits and to have more choice in taming the dragon.

STEP ONE

Identifying the Triggers (When):

Identifying your ULP in time and space is the first step to breaking through to a higher level of well-being. We'll focus first on what is occurring now so we'll know where changes may need to take place. Make an ULP section in your journal. Over the next week see what you can discover about the following.

- Notice what happens after a period of feeling really good. For example, many people have noticed the following sequence. First comes the thought, "I don't know if I can stand everything going so well much longer," then something happens to deflate the good times.
- Notice your thoughts and experience just as the happiness rolls over into a sense of dissatisfaction. Is there a particular time when these experiences seem to occur? For example, many couples specialize in what we call "The Friday Night Fights" in anticipation of an intimate weekend together.
- Study any pattern of times of noticing more critical thoughts about your partner. One couple noticed that criticism most often erupted in the late evenings. Before they made their ULP chart they hadn't realized how frequently they became critical just before bedtime and the potential for sex.
- Over the week see if the timing of your ULP pattern produces

a particular form when you plot the connected highs and lows. For example, some people build up a good feeling steadily over time, then lose it suddenly. Their pattern would look like going off a cliff. Other people may have little bursts of feeling good, followed by the strong comments of a loud critical inner voice that they do battle with. Their ULP might look like bumps in the road.

STEP TWO

Noting Your Favorite Upper-Limits Behaviors (What)

Here are some examples of specific activities people have noticed that invariably bring them down. *It is important to notice if these behaviors occur when you are feeling great and things are going well.*

- Be aware, if you or your partner starts an argument, that this is *the* most popular way to sabotage times of intimacy and good feeling.
- Notice when worry thoughts, about self, kids, work, etc., arise.
- See if you change the subject when energy is sparkling between you.
- Be aware if your ULP involves body metaphors, such as bumping into things. (This is Kathlyn's favorite. Gay can always tell that Kathlyn has had an unusually good week when he'll ask, "Where did you get that bruise?" and Kathlyn answers, "Gee, I don't remember getting it.")
- See if anyone else in the family is the designated upper-limits switch. For example, one couple was beginning to get closer after several years of conflict; then their teenage son started getting into trouble at school.
- Observe whether you create environmental ULP. For example, several couples have noticed what we call the Plumbing Issue as a favorite way to come out of feeling harmonious. The husband calls from work to invite the wife to dinner to celebrate his

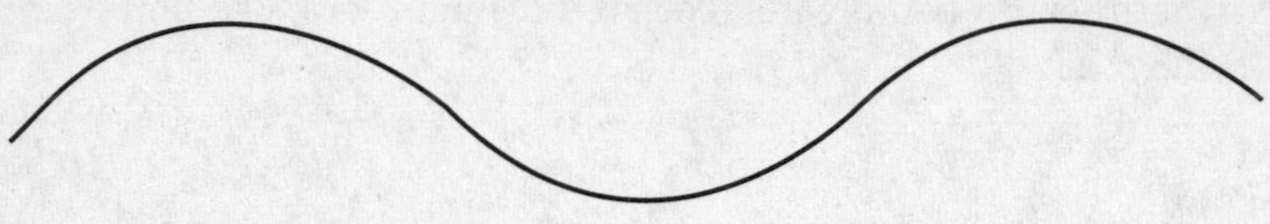

successful project, and she says, "Thank goodness you called. The toilet is backed up again."

- Notice repeated physical patterns that decrease your feeling good and when these occur. Some examples are: getting sick before an important presentation, feeling too sleepy to make love to an interested partner, and accidents.

The rising and falling line that appears above represents a typical cycle. When you have identified your favorite upper-limits strategies, take some time to chart these behaviors in the appropriate places along the line. Usually the down cycle will begin just as good feeling is peaking, although we've worked with people who anticipate good times by bringing themselves down before it gets to be too much.

STEP THREE

Finding the Source of the Pattern

One at a time, take a look at your ULP behaviors and the particular times they tend to arise. Note down your feelings and responses as you ask yourself these questions for each behavior.

"Why is this issue coming up at this time?"

"What might I be moving into or exploring if I weren't engaged in this problem?"

For example, one couple who had been separated for several years had decided, as a result of their therapy work, to move back together. In this session we were looking at the specific tasks and agreements that were needed to support the move by the first of the month. As Vince agreed to clean out years of accumulated stuff to make space for Linda to have her own separate room (e.g., thirty years of *National Geographic* magazines), we noticed Linda becoming more and more angry. She sighed, sniffed, and greeted each suggestion with a sarcastic remark. We asked her, "Why is this anger coming up at this time?" At first, she resisted any hint that her anger might have some relationship to the possibility of life working better. After several snorting retorts, she actually considered the question. She immediately recognized that anger was her habitual defense against life working. She had learned early in life that good times were fleeting, but that struggle and hard work were constants. As her face softened, Linda said, "I'm really afraid to try something new. I can't believe that Vince is really more interested in our relationship than his archives and doing things a set way. If I get huffy at least I feel I have some control. But I see I really don't have much fun that way."

TAMING YOUR UPPER-LIMITS DRAGON

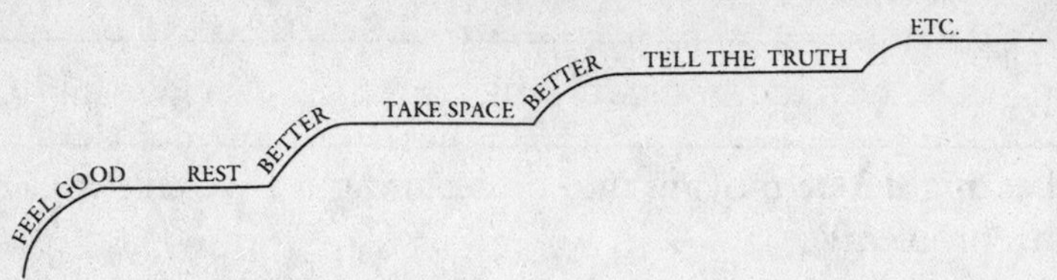

STEP FOUR

Changing Upper-Limits Patterns

Take each upper-limits behavior in your chart and design an activity you can do instead. Then when you recognize that your ULP has emerged you can make a conscious choice to do something different. You will actually be creating new pathways for joy and aliveness instead of trudging down the same old ruts. While still honoring the ebb and flow of energy, you can create a smoother flow for growth. Over time, the up-down rollercoaster of the upper-limits problem can change to: feel good, rest and integrate, feel better, take space.

On a daily basis, the following techniques are helpful in enlightening relationships:

- Take plenty of time off from the relationship. A close relationship is powerfully transformative, and you need lots of rest time to integrate the learnings from it.
- Tell the microscopic truth, especially about what is going on in your body.
- Let the other person (and yourself) go through complete energy cycles. If the other person is sad, support them in crying to completion. Don't try to help them feel better,

help them feel more deeply the emotion they are experiencing.

- Give each other plenty of nonsexual touching. Sex is great, of course, but many people do not give as much attention to nonsexual touching. We all need touch in large quantities.
- After periods of intense intimacy, get grounded in a positive way, such as through massage, a walk, dancing, completing important communications, or cleaning up your desk.
- Have at least three friends who will call you on your act, gently remind you that you create your reality, and remind you to breathe and open up to love once again.

Here are some examples of changes people have made in their upper-limits behavior.

- *Worry thoughts:* "When I notice myself worrying about money, I take a deep breath and repeat in my mind, 'I am wealthy in my life, in my family's closeness, and in my friends.' "
- *Changing the subject:* "I don't always catch myself changing the subject, but when I do I pause and take two breaths to notice what I'm really feeling. I've noticed that I'm usually scared about things being too good and spinning out of control. It's amazing—I just say that, and my fear dissolves!' "
- *Body metaphors:* Kathlyn uses the clue of bumping into things to remember to take some time off from being supercompetent and to nurture her body directly. She says that she's learned her body is saying, "Pay attention to me!" at those times, so she'll get a massage, soak in the hot tub, give herself a facial, as more positive ways to attend to herself.
- *Starting arguments:* Glenda and Rob have an agreement now that whenever an argument begins on Friday night, they will change their physical position, take several belly breaths, and rigorously practice telling the unarguable truth until they uncover the source of the ULP.
- *Environmental metaphors:* The unconscious can be quite creative in bringing subtle issues to awareness. The authors discovered an interesting, if inconvenient, environmental ULP. After several vacations and creative working trips, we came home to discover

a problem in the pipes. Once when we returned from a great trip to Hawaii we found several water pipes had burst at the mountain house. Another time all the drains in the kitchen had backed up. The third time, when the sewer line backed up after our most successful road trip, we said, "Humm. This looks like an upper-limits pattern to us." We got clear that we were willing to move into higher levels of positive energy, and not let any flow problems bring us down, and, so far, that problem has not recurred.

- *Physical patterns:* Gloria noticed that several times a year, she would get sick just before a major presentation at work. She explored this as a possible ULP, and discovered that she was repeating her get-sick response to skipping a grade and going into a new, more creative, but strange classroom. She was amazed to see that her life was still being guided by an eight-year-old. From her exploration, she invented a new strategy. When she found out a project would be due soon, she blocked out a little time each day to spend dialoguing with her inner child. She found that just ten minutes of being with and loving the scared eight-year-old freed her of the current pattern. At last report, she was having lots of fun inventing new presentation styles and getting great feedback from customers.

Use the following space to list your upper-limits patterns and the alternate activity you've designated.

UPPER-LIMITS PATTERN	NEW BEHAVIOR

________________________ ________________________

________________________ ________________________

________________________ ________________________

________________________ ________________________

ACTIVITIES FOR ENHANCING A RELATIONSHIP THAT ALREADY WORKS

We love to work with couples who come in to increase their intimacy. They say something like, "We get along really well, but we want to know if there's a possibility of having an even better time." Such folks are rare and precious. We appreciate their commitment to joy and the unlimited potential of close relationships.

If you are one of those special couples, these activities are for you.

The Four Essentials

In a recent workshop with couples, we focused on the concept of having it all. Can your relationship be large enough to encompass the four things that seem to motivate people: God, glory, gold, and spice? Historically, these four things have moved people to action, often across continents and seas. Is your search primarily about spirituality, money, fame, or variety? This activity will give you a chance to see how your relationship scales are weighted and to compare notes with your partner.

INSTRUCTIONS:

Each of you take a large sheet of blank paper and draw a line down the middle of the page. On the left-hand side of the page, write these four headings: God, Glory, Gold, and Spice. Working separately at first, list how it is, how you currently spend your time in each of these areas.

EXAMPLE:

Mary's beginning list:

GOD	GLORY	GOLD	SPICE
church on Sunday	present new material for work 1x/ month	money into IRA	pretty routine
meditate		college costs	new dress
read spiritual books			
prayer group			

Ken's beginning list:

GOD	GLORY	GOLD	SPICE
long walks	head of department	bonus this year	good sex
	written up in co. newsletter	college drains	travel
	invented new product		learning new skill

When you feel these columns are complete, write the same four headings on the right-hand side of the page, and focus on what you want, how you *want* to be spending your time.

EXAMPLE:

Mary's list:

GOD	GLORY	GOLD	SPICE
teach Sunday school	promotion at work	a private fund	less routine
	more independence	more left over	learning new skills

Ken's list:

GOD	GLORY	GOLD	SPICE
quiet times	this is great now	more left over	more sex
		gifts for Mary	class in drawing

When each of you is finished with the two lists, sit down together and compare notes. Share what has been most satisfying in each area and where you would like to bring more focus to a certain area. You may be surprised, as Mary and Ken were, to discover the areas where things match and the areas where differing interests could be a potential source of conflict. In Ken and Mary's relationship their spiritual emphases had been the seed for friction for years. As they looked at their own balances and the balance of these areas in their marriage, they saw that they met more easily in the areas of spice and gold than of glory and God.

Together, as Ken and Mary did, ask yourselves how you can support your partner to realize the items on their want list. For example, Ken saw that he could use Sunday mornings as his quiet time, to take a long walk or experience his inner life while Mary was at church, rather than doing maintenance chores around the house and then feeling resentful. Mary was a little hesitant about taking a drawing class with Ken, but discovered she could take calligraphy on the same night that Ken's drawing class was offered.

Increasing Your Spice Quotient

The following activity is designed to increase the variety in close relationship. It counteracts the tendency to use relationship as an excuse to nestle into the status quo and gently snooze. Successful relationships are large enough to embrace change in both partners and actually thrive on the new energy change brings to them.

Here are some signs that you are taking the other for granted or nestling into repetition:

- Mind wandering when your partner is speaking
- Assumptions about what your partner should or shouldn't do for you
- Interpretations and judgments about how your partner chooses to spend time
- Frequent upsets when something unexpected changes the daily schedule
- Resentment about daily routines
- Realizing that you've heard these stories many times before
- Frequent fantasizing about other romantic partners, especially in times of intimacy
- Protesting suggestions about learning something new together, such as dancing

Take a few minutes to see if any of these symptoms are familiar. Looking at this list may remind you of other similar signs in your relationship. Would you be willing to increase the spice quotient in your relationship? If so, read on.

INSTRUCTIONS:

STEP ONE

Each of you complete the following sentences.

- Every day for the last week, I've ______________.

  (e.g., gotten up at 6:45 with the alarm and stumbled into the shower.)

- I need to have ______________ each day.

  (e.g., dinner at 6:30; all the beds made before I will do something fun.)

- I get upset when my partner doesn't regularly __________.

  (e.g., clean up after him/herself immediately.)

- I get upset when my partner always ______________.

  (e.g., brings unexpected guests home from work; waits for me to discipline the kids.)

- When unexpected things happen, I feel ______________.

  (e.g., scared that things are going to spin out of control.)

STEP TWO

Look over your list and choose one routine that you would be willing to change by spicing it up. For example, you may be willing to add variety in your work-before-play routine for making the beds. Invent a way to change the way you structure this aspect of your life. Then invent another that may seem totally outrageous or silly. Then invent several more.

Example:

- I will make the beds upside down.
- I will paint first thing in the morning and then make the beds.

- We'll get large sleeping bags and not make the beds at all.
- I'll sing opera-style while I make my bed, demanding in a loud voice that the kids make their beds before breakfast.
- I'll make the kids' beds and they'll make mine.

Look at your list and ask, Which of these possible changes am I willing to try for this week? The one that makes you smile inside is probably a good choice. Let yourself have a week's experimental time with this new way of doing things and then evaluate the level of spiciness in your life. At the end of the week, choose another item from your list and proceed through Step Two with it. We recommmend starting with items that concern you individually before moving to items that involve your relationship.

Moving Together in Harmony

Our structured, technologically grounded lives don't often provide space for partners to experience the joys of moving together. This simple but powerful activity is a favorite in our seminars. Each person gets a chance to lead and to follow. Partners' faces light up after sharing this unusual way of walking together. You'll need enough space to walk around comfortably. Some couples like to do this activity outdoors.

INSTRUCTIONS:

Decide who will be the first leader and who the first follower. (If you're feeling metaphorical, call one the engine and one the caboose.) Start by standing. The leader will have eyes open throughout the activity.

Follower, stand directly behind the leader and rest your hands easily on each side at her/his lower ribs or waist area. Take a moment to feel the expansion and contraction of each breath through your hands. Stand close enough so that your elbows are bent. This is a standing form of the spoon position. Follower, gently close your eyes and leave them closed throughout the activity.

Leader, slowly and rhythmically, shift your weight from side to side. Sway for several minutes until you feel your partner flowing right along with you. Sometimes as you begin this activity, little jerks and starts occur, but as partners synchronize breath and movement, it is sometimes difficult to tell who is initiating.

Leader, when you feel that the follower is comfortable and moving with you, begin to take tiny steps with each shift of your weight. Move slowly at first, until you feel harmonized with the follower. After a few moments you can begin moving around the room with larger steps. If a hitch occurs and jerky motion results, shift back to swaying together until harmony is restored. Some partners enjoy fancy variations at this point, such as moving backward; turning; inserting glides, skips, and other more complex steps; or speeding up and slowing down. These additions are optional; if you want, create more together.

When you come to a good stopping place, rest for a moment and then switch roles.

Dream Sharing

One of the deepest pleasures of a close, transparent relationship is the experience of discovering and sharing the bottomless well of each other's inner worlds. As a couple, we share this realm in several ways each day, through meditation, breathing together, and telling the truth about our ongoing process. A particularly delicious way we want to recommend is to share your dreams when you awaken.

The simple act of expressing a dream image or sequence is simultaneously liberating and grounding. It clears the cloudy hangover that visits to the unconscious sometimes generate. It can also bring shadow issues to the surface in a friendlier way than having them show up in an argument or as illness. For example, on a recent vacation Kathlyn woke out of a dream that Gay was leaving her, despite her pleas, "Don't you see that this is an upper-limit problem?" Our first response was some hilarity that our relationship lingo had filtered so deeply into the unconscious. After sharing more of the feeling tone and images of the dream, Kathlyn realized that she was afraid of leaving herself in some fundamental way, splitting away from the incredible happiness that is an ongoing reality now.

Sharing your dreams allows you to dip into the underground currents that are continually evolving in each of you and your life together. For example, we have often found that a dream image shared in the morning shows up in a different form later in the day. Or the dream is completed by an event we couldn't have predicted. Not long ago Gay shared a dream image of his mother closing up the house to move away. Gay's mother died in 1990 after a long illness, and the house had been on the market since. A week or so after this dream he signed a solid contract for the sale of the house. Perhaps he had completed some aspect of his relationship with his mother or let go of the associations that the house held. In any case, his dream sharing brought that unconscious image to the light of day.

INSTRUCTIONS:

Use the following questions as guidelines for your dream sharing. Feel free to amend or add to them as you grow in your dream life together.

- What emotion is most predominant in the dream?
- List the dream images you remember (don't worry about recalling everything).
- What is the feeling tone of the dream: misty, sharp, heavy and sad, epic?
- What is the flow of action, or process, in the dream?
- Are any objects very large or unusually small in the dream?
- Is there any part of the dream that you feel hesitant to share? Take a look at that and explore what truth can be told here.
- Does the dream seem complete to you, or unfinished? If unfinished, how might you complete it?
- As you share, let yourself be aware of any other images, thoughts or feelings that pop into your mind. Express them also.

Fluffing the Body Energy

This activity is designed to lighten up your interactions and create new ways to play together. We call it fluffing because the most effective relationship tool is space. When we fluff an issue or possibility, new options emerge. This activity is the opposite of "working on it." For that reason partners use it to heighten their fun level together.

Fluffing Option One:

Decide who will be the fluffer and who the fluffee. Fluffee, take a moment to notice where your body feels most dense or tight right now. Identify the place for the fluffer. Both of you will fluff at the same time, in different ways. Fluffee, do your best to fluff the area with your breath. Fluffer, use your hands on this part as if you were fluffing a pillow behind someone's head. Continue fluffing until the area feels lighter and more spacious. Then switch roles.

Fluffing Option Two:

The fluffee is lying down for this activity. Identify an area of your body where you would like some attention. You may want to love this part of you more, or bring more awareness to an area that speaks to you with pain or tension. Fluffer, your job is to fluff this part by humming it. Use your closed mouth against the part and hum at different pitches until you find the one that vibrates your partner most pleasurably. That may be signaled by giggles, wiggling, or a smile appearing at the corners of the fluffee's mouth. When your partner is nicely fluffed, switch roles.

Fluffing Option Three:

Sit back to back so that each of you is equally supported and comfortable. Breathe together with the intention of fluffing each other's back. Let your breath fluff all the way through each of you.

Fluffing Option Four:

Stand facing each other. Take turns noticing and appreciating something about your partner. Pause between each appreciation for two breaths. Let yourself move and expand as you receive each appreciation. Continue until each of you feels well fluffed.

Supporting Creativity

In this activity we want to share some of the ways we have discovered to enhance each other's creativity. We invite you to add to the list. Choose one item and focus on it until you have incorporated it into your lifestyle. Then move to another.

- At frequent intervals, ask, "What do you want?" We ask this question for many different areas of life: the material realm, spiritual goals, learning experiences, adventures, etc. And we listen carefully to the response. Inquiring about and expressing your leading edge empowers its fulfillment.
- Ask, "How can I support you in your goals?" Listen to the response and make agreements about your support.
- Ask, "What are you curious about today? What are you interested in learning or exploring?" Listen to the response and see if there are any concrete actions that would support your partner's interest.

- Support your partner in having a regular solo time to explore her/his interests and creative play. That time is sacred and needs to be honored, whether it's a half-hour meditation time or the two hours we spend separately writing and creating each morning. Each of you study what times of day are your peak creative times and protect them. The highest levels of creation are between you and the universe.
- Interrupt routines when you notice them dulling your life sparkle (see activity in Problem-Solving section).
- Schedule time for the "necessary but trivial" elements of your life together so that household and business items don't ooze out and cover the whole day in details.
- Look at your environment and explore how you can invite creativity by the colors and space you live in. For example, change the arrangement of things and furniture at intervals; have creative toys available, such as musical instruments, drums, stuffed animals, balls, paint and paper, etc.; create uncluttered open spaces to relax in; redecorate your work and play areas in colors that promote relaxation; explore what environmental ambience supports creativity. For example, do you prefer music in the background or quiet, uninterrupted time?

Afterword

....

We have come now to the end of the activities and of our time together. As therapists we have been privileged to be with hundreds of people as they have created the kinds of relationships they wanted. We have been with hundreds of couples who were working to transform their relationships into something closer to their hearts' desire. Now as we send these powerful tools and techniques out into the world through the medium of this book, we want to thank all of the people who made it possible. To thank them by name would be impossible, but they will know who they are. They will always live in our hearts. We also want to give thanks in advance to all of you who will read this book and put it to use in your relationships. May your relationship journey be as richly blessed as ours has been.

Our own relationship has been the greatest beneficiary of the material in the book. Through employing the ideas in our own lives, we have grown in creativity and love beyond our wildest dreams. What most excites us now is seeing others discover the power and possibilities of these new ways of being. As you take these ideas and craft them to fit your life, it is our hope that you use them as an evolutionary springboard to ever higher states of happiness and harmony. In the realm of relationship, there is no ceiling to the amount of love and creativity you can enjoy. It is our hope that you will revel in the boundless love at the center of yourself, celebrate it in others, and raise the art of intimacy to a height hitherto unknown on Planet Earth.

Index